THE EXPANSION OF THE COMMON LAW.

BY

SIR FREDERICK POLLOCK, BART., D.C.L.,

HON. LL.D., BARRISTER-AT-LAW,

Corresponding Member of the Institute of France; late Corpus Professor of Jurisprudence, Oxford; past Fellow of Trinity College, Cambridge;

Author of "PRINCIPLES OF CONTRACT," "THE LAW OF TORTS,"

etc., etc.

THE LAWBOOK EXCHANGE, LTD.

Union, New Jersey

2002

ISBN 1-58477-169-0

Third printing 2004

Printed in the United States of America
on acid-free paper

The Lawbook Exchange, Ltd.
33 Terminal Avenue
Clark, New Jersey 07066-1321

Please see our website
www.lawbookexchange.com
for a selection of our other publications and fine facsimile reprints
of classic works of legal history.

Library of Congress Cataloging-in-Publication Data

Pollock, Frederick, Sir, 1845-1937.
The expansion of the common law / by Sir Frederick Pollock. p. cm.
Originally published: London: Stevens, 1904.
Includes bibliographical references and index.
ISBN 1-58477-169-0 (cloth: alk. paper)
1. Common law. I. Title.

K588 .P649 2001
340.5'7—dc2l 00-0670 15

THE EXPANSION OF THE COMMON LAW.

BY

SIR FREDERICK POLLOCK, BART., D.C.L.,

HON. LL.D., BARRISTER-AT-LAW,

Corresponding Member of the Institute of France; late Corpus Professor of Jurisprudence, Oxford; past Fellow of Trinity College, Cambridge;

Author of "PRINCIPLES OF CONTRACT," "THE LAW OF TORTS,"

etc., etc.

LONDON:

STEVENS AND SONS, LIMITED,

119 & 120, CHANCERY LANE,

Law Publishers.

1904.

LONDON:

PRINTED BY C. F. ROWORTH, GREAT NEW STREET, FETTER LANE, E.C.

TO

FREDERIC WILLIAM MAITLAND.

Kinder werfen den Ball an die Wand und fangen ihn wieder:
Aber ich lobe das Spiel, wirft mir der Freund ihn zurück.

GOETHE: *Vier Jahreszeiten.*

PREFACE.

The lectures from which this volume is named were delivered to the Law Schools of several American Universities last autumn. A few additions have been made to the original text. The address given at the request of the Harvard Law School Association for its commemoration of 1895 was not intended at the time to have any sequel, but is now prefixed to the course of 1903 as being sufficiently germane to the matter to serve as a general introduction.

Familiar matters of both fact and law were necessarily taken for granted in delivering the lectures; and it does not now seem desirable to vouch authorities at large for them. References have been given only where it is thought that they may be really useful for verification or farther search.

Taking a rapid survey of a wide field, I have left the learned reader to supply for himself many qualifications which it would have been proper to express if I had been writing at greater length. Students will do well to bear this in mind for their own sake, and I hope critical scholars will do the like for the author's. Nothing in nature is absolutely black or white, but a sketch in black and white may be faithful to the extent of its means, and my aim has been of that kind.

F. P.

LINCOLN'S INN,

Whitsuntide, 1904.

CONTENTS.

THE

VOCATION OF THE COMMON LAW (a).

TWELVE years ago, before I had formed any definite purpose of seeing with my own eyes and hearing with my own ears how the Common Law prospers on this side of the ocean, I exhorted those who heard my first lecture at Oxford to embrace all opportunities of greeting with no stranger's welcome those brethren from the West who come to visit our ancient seats of learning in the name of our common tongue and common doctrine. Converting Scripture to the use of the moment in a manner which would have needed no justification or excuse for a medieval lawyer, I then made bold to say: "Benedictus qui venit in nomine legum Angliae." Since that time I have done what little I could do to fulfil my own precept; little enough, in any case, in comparison of the reward. For within a year I found myself here, and I knew that the blessing had come back to me by this token among others: to wit, that before my acquaintance with my learned friend the Royall Professor was a quarter of an hour old we were deep in the question whether determinable estates in fee simple are known to the Common Law, and if so what are

(a) An Address delivered at the Commemoration meeting of the Harvard Law School Association, June 25, 1895.

the properties of such an estate. Now I am again here, this time at your express bidding. The honour you have been pleased to do me is, as regards myself, one of the most gratifying I have ever received. But I should fail to esteem it at its full worth if I were to take it as confined to my own person, and did not accept it as a mark of your friendly affection and remembrance addressed in this hour of your festal gathering to the Bar and the Universities of the old country. And, as in private duty bound, I must especially rejoice in the office to which you have called me as being a fresh visible sign of the original bond that links this University, in name and in substance, with my own University of Cambridge in England. Standing on that venerable bond as a sufficient authority, I hold myself well entitled, here and now, to wish Harvard and its Law School continuance and increase of all good things in the name both of the profession at home and of the humanities which you most wisely deem an essential preparation for the study of the law.

It would be an idle task for me to praise the aims or the work of the Harvard Law School in this presence. For, although it would in truth be sincere, praise coming from your guest could not be above the suspicion of partiality for any one who chose to suspect, nor therefore could it carry much weight with any one still standing in need of conviction. Still less would it befit this occasion to enter into a controversial discussion of actual or possible methods of legal instruction. Even if this Law School were not past the stage of apologetics, it would be an impertinence not to suppose you better prepared to defend your own system, and better capable of judging the time, season, and manner of any defence, than the most sympathetic of strangers. There is one product of your School, however, that stands apart and can be judged on its independent merits: I mean the Harvard Law Review. Now this Review has been in existence only eight years, and within that time its contributions to the history and science of our law have been of the utmost value. This is so far from being controvertible that it can hardly be called matter of opinion at all. No such record of profitable activity has been shown within recent times by any other law school; and although it is not necessary to commit oneself to the correctness of this statement beyond the range of English-speaking countries, I do not know that there would be any great rashness in making it universal. The singularly full and brilliant number of the Review published in honour of Dean Langdell's silver wedding with the School need not fear comparison with the festival collections of essays produced at any German University. The school that commands the services of such teachers and workers is at all events a living power. Let us pass on to consider in what manner of sphere it works.

The fact of such a meeting as the present implies a greater matter than the merits of even the best law school, Harvard has sent out her sons to practise in the courts of many jurisdictions, and they return to her in no way estranged. Coming from England myself, I am here, as a lawyer, more at home than in Scotland. We are not a congress come together to compare notes of different systems, if haply we may understand one another and profit by an exchange of novel wares; we are not only of one speech but of one rule; we talk freely of *our* law, the Common Law. This is one of the things we do so naturally that it seems too simple for discussion. And yet it is among the wonders of history, and may be not wholly without philosophical bearings. If, as a certain school would have it, law be merely the command of a sovereign power, that which the legislature of Massachusetts, or New York, or the United Kingdom, has thought fit to ordain or permit; if law be this and nothing more, then it would seem that the historical and empirical coincidences between the commands it has pleased our respective political sovereigns to issue deserve much less importance than we have been accustomed to attach to them, and that there is no rational justification for your habit (existing, I believe, in all or nearly all the States) of citing English decisions more frequently than those of any other external jurisdiction (*a*). If on the other hand our traditions, our professional habits of thought, and our judicial practice are not foolishness, it would seem to be because law is not an affair of bare literal precepts, as the mechanical school would make it, but is the sense of justice taking form in peoples and races. The law of our English-speaking commonwealths on which the sun never sets is one law in many varieties, not many laws which happen to resemble one another in several particulars.

Historians and publicists may discuss how far the political separation of these States from the British Crown was beneficial to the mother country and the emancipated family, what drawbacks were incident on either side to the advantages, and how far they were avoidable or not so. Lawyers may join them in regretting that the hostilities which at one time actually took place between the United States and the French Republic were not prolonged or not

(*a*) See Harv. Law Rev. viii. 501-2.

serious enough to bring about an Anglo-American alliance. For in that event we should not only have escaped the war of 1812, and learnt to respect one another as comrades instead of adversaries in arms; not only might some great fraternal victory have anticipated Trafalgar, and the Napoleonic legend have been cut short in its career of mischief; but the exploits of our combined naval strength would have directed the combined intellect of British and American jurists to the definition and improvement of public law. The law of nations would have been enriched with results, possibly of greater intrinsic merit, assuredly of more commanding authority, than any that we have yet seen. But a common enmity—which in this case turned out, as regards the United States, to arise from transitory causes—was not enough to found an alliance within so short a time of the first embittered separation. Anyhow, there is little profit to be had from straying into the dream-land of events that did not happen. And if any one should go so far on this line as to regret not only the manifestly regrettable incidents of our separation, but the fact that the independence of the United States was established fully, clearly, and absolutely, I do not see how any of us, whether American or English, can be free as a lawyer to go along with him. For without this perfect independence of local sovereignty and jurisdiction it would never have been made known how deep and firm is the organic unity of our legal institutions and science, which the shock of severance and a century of independent judicial and legislative activity have left, in all essential features, untouched.

We need no witnesses, least of all in an assembly of lawyers, to prove the persistence of this unity. But on this western side of the ocean it is more conspicuous than on the eastern. The very multifariousness of tribunals and legislatures under a federal constitution drives you back from the varying details of practice in this and that State to seek the fountain-head of principle in the central ideas of the law. To guide and encourage this process is among the functions of the Supreme Court of the United States; we need not attempt to measure it against the high constitutional and political duties assigned to that Court, but at all events it is mainly in virtue of this office that the Court is not only renowned but influential far beyond the borders of its actual jurisdiction. Even the Supreme Court of the United States, however, must in the long run be what the training and temper of the legal profession make it. And, if we are to know what the profession at its best will be in the coming generation, we still have to look among those who are teaching and learning. If there be any seat of learning where this ideal of the essential unity of the Common Law in all its dwelling-places has been wisely and diligently cherished, it is Harvard; if there be any teacher whose work has been steadfastly directed to this end, it is Mr. Langdell, whose long and excellent service to this School, and not only to this School, we are now happy to celebrate.

Mr. Langdell has insisted, as we all know, on the importance of studying law at first hand in the actual authorities. I am not sure whether this is the readiest way to pass examinations; that is as the questions and the examiners may be. I do feel sure it is the best way, if not the only one, to learn law. By pointing out that way Mr. Langdell has done excellently well. But the study he has inculcated by precept and example is not a mere letter-worship of authority. No man has been more ready than Mr. Langdell to protest against the treatment of conclusions of law as something to be settled by mere enumeration of decided points. For the law is not a collection of propositions, but a system founded on principles; and although judicial decisions are in our system the best evidence of the principles, yet not all decisions are acceptable or ultimately accepted, and principle is the touchstone by which particular decisions have to be tried. Decisions are made, principles live and grow. This conviction is at the root of all Mr. Langdell's work, and makes his criticism not only keen but vital. Others can give us rules; he gives us the method and the power that can test the reason of rules. And therefore, as it seems to me, his work has been of a singularly fruitful kind, and profitable out of proportion to its visible bulk. Probably several of us have dissented, now and again, from this or that opinion of Mr. Langdell's. We may have been unable to concur in his deduction, or we may have thought that his reasoning was correct, but the received authorities were too strongly against him, and that he must be content with standing as the Cato of a vanquished cause. But none of us, I think, has ever failed to learn something even when he could not follow. For my own part, I have considered and reconsidered much of Mr. Langdell's criticism; I have more than once, on a second or third time of reflection, come round to think with him; at all times, whether going side by side with Mr. Langdell or withstanding him, I have felt, and the feeling has grown upon me with riper acquaintance, that appreciation of his point of view was sure to bring one nearer to the heart of the Common Law.

Now it may be said, and truly, that the range of any

one man's work, even the best, is limited. We have to see whether it is typical, one of like examples present and to come. Permanent fruits can be assured only when the stock is multiplied. In the case before us we are encouraged in no small degree by the fact that Mr. Langdell stands eminent but by no means alone. The same spirit in which he has taught and criticized has been carried by others not only into the literary exposition but into the judicial development of the law. The name of my friend Mr. Justice Holmes will already be in your minds. In England we can perhaps speak, for the moment, less cheerfully. We are still lamenting the loss of two great judges who most worthily represented this universal and unifying spirit of our law (and I may the more fitly mention them here because you knew them), Lord Hannen and Lord Bowen. That loss is all the greater because the besetting danger of modern law is the tendency of complex facts and minute legislation to leave no room for natural growth, and to choke out the life of principles under a weight of dead matter which posterity may think no better than a rubbish-heap. And the continued divorce of the academical from the practical study of law in the old country is not, in my opinion, a good thing either for the Universities or for the Inns of Court. Nevertheless the main stream runs clear. Any one who follows the decisions of the House of Lords and the Court of Appeal from year to year will be satisfied, I think, that the science of law is still as much alive in England as ever; and, so far as my opportunities of knowledge have gone, I think you will be ready to warrant me in saying the same of the United States. Only we need, it seems to me, a little more self-confidence, a further touch of the quality that Mr. Swinburne has somewhere called "an excellent arrogance." Our medieval ancestors were certainly not lacking in this quality; they might have done well, perhaps, if they could have saved a little of their superfluity for us. I will endeavour to explain my meaning.

We have long given up the attempt to maintain that the Common Law is the perfection of reason. Existing human institutions can only do their best with the conditions they work in. If they can do that within the reasonable margin to be allowed for mistakes and accidents, they are justified in their generation. Even their ideal is relative. What is best for one race or one society, at a given stage of civilization, is not necessarily best for other races and societies at other stages. We cannot say that one set of institutions is in itself better or more reasonable than another, except with reference express or implied to conditions that are assumed either to be universal in human societies, or to be not materially different in the particular cases compared. It may perhaps be safe to assume, in a general way, that what is reasonable for Massachusetts is reasonable for Vermont. It would not be at all safe to assume that everything reasonable for Massachusetts is reasonable for British India, nor, indeed, that within British India what will serve for Lower Bengal will equally well serve for the north-west frontier. The first right of every system, therefore, is to be judged in its own field, by its own methods, and on its own work. It cannot be seen at its best, or even fairly, if its leading conceptions are forced into conformity with an alien mould. A sure mark of the mere handicraftsman is to wonder how foreigners can get on with tools in any way different from his own. Thus in England one shall meet people who cannot understand that the Scots do without any formal difference between law and equity; as, on the other hand, I have known learned Scots fail to perceive that the Common Law doctrine of consideration, being unknown to the law of Scotland, is yet founded on a hard bottom of economic fact which every legal system has to strike somewhere. We now realize that the laws of every nation are determined by their own historical conditions not only as to details but as to structure; and if we fail to attend to this we cannot duly appreciate the system as we find it at a given time. Many points of early Roman law remain obscure to us, notwithstanding more than half a century of the brilliant and devoted work of modern scholars, just because the historical conditions are matter of conjecture. In our own system the most elementary phrases of equity jurisprudence carry with them a vast burden of judicial and political conflict; and the range of activity left open to the Court of Chancery in Blackstone's time can be understood only when we have mastered both the strength and the weakness of the Action on the Case two centuries earlier. But history does not exclude reason and continuity, no more than a man's parentage and companions prevent him from having a character of his own. Development is a process and not a succession of incidents. Environment limits and guides the direction of effort; it cannot create the living growth.

Hence it seems to follow that a system which is vital and really individual either must be resigned to remain in some measure inarticulate, or must have some account to give of itself that is not merely dogmatic and not merely external history, but combines the rational and the historical element. In other words, its aims are not completely achieved unless it has a philosophy; and that philosophy must be its own. This we recognize freely enough as regards other systems. It appears to us quite natural that Roman law should have its proper conceptions and terminology. We think no worse of the Roman law of property for starting from the conception of absolute ownership rather than the conception of estates, no worse of the Roman law of injuries by negligence for being developed by way of commentary on a specific statute, and not, as with us, through judicial analogies of the simpler notion of Trespass, aided by statute only so far as the Statute of Westminster was necessary for the existence of actions on the case. What I desire to suggest is that, as we allow this liberty to others as matter of right, we should not be afraid of claiming it for ourselves; that, if English-speaking lawyers are really to believe in their own science, they must seek a genuine philosophy of the Common Law and not be put off with a surface dressing of Romanized generalities.

Take for example the Germanic idea which lies at the root of our whole law of property, the idea of Seisin. So much has this idea been overlaid with artificial distinctions and refinements in the course of seven centuries that it is possible even for learned persons to treat it as obsolete. Nevertheless it is there still. Actual enjoyment and control of land or goods, the recognition of peaceable enjoyment and control as deserving the protection of the law, the defence of them against usurpation and, at need, restitution by the power of the State for the person who has been deprived of them by unauthorized force: these are the points that stand in the forefront of the Common Law when we take it as presented by its own history and in its native authorities. Or, more briefly, possession guaranteed by law is with us a primary, not a secondary notion. Possession and rights to possess are the subject-matter of our remedies and forms of action. The notion of ownership, as the maximum of claim or right in a specific thing allowed by law (*a*), is not primary, but developed out of conflicting claims to possession and disposal. He is the true owner who has the best right to possess, and to set or leave others in his place fortified with like rights and exercising like powers over the thing in question. This is the line of development indicated by our own authorities. It leads us gradually from the crude facts to the artificial ideas of law, from the visible will and competence of the Germanic warrior to use his arms against any intruder on his homestead to the title, rights, and priorities of the modern holder of stock or debentures. It is impossible here to follow the steps; they form a long and sometimes intricate history. But is the process on the face of it absurd? Is there anything unreasonable about it? Can one assign any obvious objection against using the genius of our own laws as the most promising guide to their fundamental ideas? As it is, our students, not to say the books they put their trust in, are in little better plight than our learned ancestors of the eighteenth century. They too commonly start with a smattering of Roman doctrine taken directly or indirectly from Justinian, then find (as they needs must) a great gulf between Roman and English methods, and lastly make desperate endeavours to span it with a sort of magic bridge by invoking supposed mysteries of feudalism which in truth are in no way to the purpose: and they are still on the wrong side when all is done. Is

(*a*) "A man cannot have a more large or greater estate of inheritance than fee simple." Litt. s. 11.

there any real need for this trouble? I venture to think not. Let us dare to be true to ourselves, and, even if the first steps seem less easy (for everybody thinks he knows by the light of nature what ownership is, and resents being undeceived), we shall find increasing light instead of gathering darkness as we go farther on the way (*a*). We may smile at our medieval ancestors' anxiety to keep something tangible to hold on to, their shrinking from incorporeal things as something uncanny, their attempts, as late as the fourteenth century, to give delivery of an advowson by the handle of the church door; their Germanic simplicity may be called rude and materialistic; but at all events they did their best to keep us in sight of living facts. In some respects they failed; we cannot deny it. It is no fault of theirs that the arbitrary legislation of the Tudor period plunged us into a turbid ocean, vexed by battles of worse than fabulous monsters, in whose depths the gleams of a *scintilla juris* may throw a darkling light on the gambols of executory limitations, a brood of coiling slippery creatures abhorred of the pure Common Law, or on the death-struggle of a legal estate sucked dry in the octopus-like arms of a resulting use; while on the surface, peradventure, a shoal of equitable remainders may be seen skimming the waves in flight from that insatiable enemy of their kind, an outstanding term. There are some ravages of history that philosophy cannot repair, and the repentance of later generations can at best only patch.

(*a*) My learned friend Prof. Holland is conspicuous among the few modern theoretical writers who have had the courage to put Possession before Ownership (Elements of Jurisprudence, ch. xi.). Mr. Henry T. Terry, in "Leading Principles of Anglo-American Law" (1884), has taken the same line yet more decidedly.

Observe that when I defend our fathers I make no pretence of right to attack the Roman institutional system on its own ground. The history of Roman forms of action and Roman legal categories is quite different from ours. The Common Law has never had a procedure answering to the Roman Vindication. At first sight it may seem a small matter whether a man who finds his cattle in strange hands shall say "Those are my beasts; it is no business of mine where you got them: I claim them because they are mine" (which is the Roman way), or shall reverse the order of thought and say "Where did you get those beasts? for they were mine, and you have no business to hold them against me" (which is the Germanic way). Practically, no doubt, the result may come to much the same thing; but the divergence of method goes pretty deep. The formulas of the Roman republican period are already more modern and abstract than ours, and the Roman lawyers of the Empire, when they began to systematize, had to construct their system accordingly. The fact that their work, in its main lines, has lasted to this day, and has stamped itself on the modern codes of not only Latin but Teutonic nations, is enough to show that it was not ill done. Only when modern admirers claim universal speculative supremacy for the Roman ideas and methods need we feel called upon to protest. In that case we must remind the too zealous Romanizer that the masters of modern Roman law, notwithstanding their advantages in systematic training and in having a comparatively manageable bulk of material, are still not much nearer than ourselves to the attainment of an unanimous or decisive last word on Possession, or Ownership, or divers other fundamental topics.

One might produce further examples to show the danger of being in haste to abandon our own methods, and the still greater dangers that arise from well-meant attempts to improve them by mixing them with others. Thus our native Common Law Procedure is in essence contentious; it is a combat between parties in which the Court is only umpire. Our equity procedure, a sufficiently acclimatized exotic but still an exotic, is in essence officious; it represents (though one cannot say that in modern times it has actually been) an active inquiry by the Court, aimed at extracting the truth of the matter in the Court's own way. No one has put this contrast on record more clearly or forcibly than Mr. Langdell. Twenty years ago the authors of our Judicature Acts in England, men of the highest eminence, but trained exclusively in the Chancery system, went about to engraft considerable parts of that system on the practice of the Courts of Common Law. What came of their good intentions? Instead of the simplicity and substantial equity which they looked for, the new birth of justice was found to be perplexed practice, vexatious interlocutory proceedings, and multiplication of appeals and costs, so that for several years the latter state of the suitor was worse than the former. Repeated revision of the Rules of Court, and some fresh legislation, was needed before the reconstructed machine would work smoothly. But I may not pursue these matters here, and can only guess that perhaps American parallels might be found. I think I have shown that the Common Law has a right to its individuality, and, if we now turn to facts observable on this continent and elsewhere in order to see how that right maintains itself in practice, I do not think we can fairly be accused of taking refuge in empiricism.

The vitality of any coherent scheme of rules or doctrine may be tested in various ways. Among other tests the power of holding or gaining ground in competition with rivals, and the faculty of assimilating new matter without being overwhelmed by it, are perhaps as good as any. We shall find, I think, that in religious and philosophical debate each advocate concerns himself to justify the system of his choice according to these tests quite as much as to establish its truth or superiority by demonstrative proof. If I may use the highest example without offence, modern theology, so far as it is apologetic and not purely critical, pays much more attention to the general standing of Christianity in relation to modern ethics and civilization than to discussing the testimony of the apostles and evangelists as if it was a series of findings by a special jury. The plain man asks not what you can prove about yourself, but what you have done and can do; and the philosopher may perhaps find more reason in this method than the plain man himself knows. Applying it to the case in hand, we see that the Common Law has had considerable opportunities and trials both in the East and in the West in presence of other systems.

In British India the general principles of our law, by a process which we may summarily describe as judicial application confirmed and extended by legislation, have in the course of this century, but much more rapidly within the last generation, covered the whole field of criminal law, civil wrongs, contract, evidence, procedure in the higher if not in the lower courts, and a good deal of the law of property. Family relations and inheritance are the remaining stronghold of the native systems of personal law, which are fortified by their intimate connexion with religious or semi-religious custom. It is not much to say that a modified English law is thus becoming the general law of British India, for if the French instead of ourselves had conquered India the same thing must have happened, only that the "justice, equity, and good conscience" by which European judges had to guide themselves in default of any other applicable rule would have been Gallican and not Anglican. But it is something to say that the Common Law has proved equal to its task. The Indian Penal Code (*a*), which is English criminal law simplified and set in order, has worked for more than a generation, among people of every degree of civilization, with but little occasion for amendment. In matters of business and commerce English law has not only established itself (*b*) but has been ratified by deliberate legislation, subject to the reform of some few anomalies which we might well have reformed at home ere now, and to the abrogation of some few rules that had ceased to be of much importance at home, and were deemed unsuitable for Indian conditions. More than this, principles of equitable jurisprudence which we seldom have occasion to remember in modern English practice have been successfully revived in Indian jurisdictions within our own time for the discomfiture of oppressive and fraudulent money-lenders. The details of procedure both civil and criminal have

(*a*) "The Indian Penal Code may be described as the criminal law of England freed from all technicalities and superfluities" [this is perhaps a little too strong], "systematically arranged and modified in some few particulars (they are surprisingly few) to suit the circumstances of British India." Stephen, Hist. Crim. Law of Eng., iii. 300.

(*b*) We cannot say that it has been received. See the section on "Natural Justice in the Common Law," p. 123, below.

undergone much revision and transformation in British India as in most other civilized countries and states: and there is doubtless much to be said of both success and failure in this department. But, since neither the praise nor the blame that may be due to modern codes of procedure can be said to touch the Common Law save in a very remote way, they do not concern us here.

There is another example in which you may take a neighbourly interest, that of the Province of Quebec. You are aware that the inhabitants of Lower Canada live in the guaranteed enjoyment of a law whose base is not English but French, and that their Civil Code, enacted not quite a generation ago, is avowedly modelled on the Code Napoléon. Nevertheless the Common Law (which of course prevails in the other provinces of the Dominion) has set its mark to some extent on the substance of legal justice in French Canada, and to a considerable extent on procedure. We find in the civil procedure of Lower Canada, as we should expect, the decisory oath of the defendant, and other features of pleading and process common to all modern systems derived from Roman law; but we also find that in a large proportion of causes either party can demand a trial by jury. This may be said to show the Common Law competing against a powerful rival under the greatest possible disadvantage, or rather making itself felt in spite of being excluded from formal competition.

Perhaps the assimilation of new matter is a yet stricter test of vital power than tenacity on old ground, or prevalence over enfeebled rivals. In this case the great example is the incorporation of the law merchant with the Common Law, and the immense development of commercial law that accompanied and followed this process. Anglicized law merchant has become to a certain extent insular; but if we must admit so much to its disadvantage, I believe it is on the other hand a wider, richer, and more flexible system than is to be found in the commercial codes of France and her imitators, who have stereotyped mercantile usage and business habits as they existed in the seventeenth century. We have indeed preserved antiquated forms, but we preserve them because every clause and almost every word carries a meaning settled by modern decisions. A policy of marine insurance is to our current maritime law somewhat as a text of the Praetor's edict to a title of the Digest built upon it. And this does not prevent further development. The courts cannot contradict what has already been settled as law, but the power of taking up fresh material is still alive, as we have been assured by high authority in England within the present generation.

Can we rest here in contemplating the past work and present activity of the Common Law? We cannot forbear, I think, to look to the future and consider what security we have for the maintenance of this vital unity. Ten years ago the Supreme Court of the United States declared, in a judgment of admirable clearness and good sense which I trust will be followed in England when the occasion comes, that in matters of general commercial principle "a diversity in the law as administered on the two sides of the Atlantic . . . is greatly to be deprecated" (*a*). Shall this remain for all time a mere deprecation, appealing forcibly, no doubt, to the best sense of our highest tribunals, but still subject to human accidents? Is there not any way, besides and beyond the discussion of

(*a*) *Norrington* v. *Wright*, 115 U. S. 89, 206.

lawyers in books and otherwise, of assisting our ultimate authorities to agree? Would not the best and surest way be that in matters of great weight, and general importance to the Common Law, they should assist one another? Certainly there are difficulties in the way of any such process: but is there in truth any insuperable difficulty? The House of Lords, as we know, is entitled to consult the judges of the land, though not bound either to consult them in any particular case or, when they are consulted, to decide according to their opinion or that of the majority. There is nothing I know of in our constitution to prevent the House of Lords, if it should think fit, from desiring the judges of the Supreme Court of the United States, by some indirect process if not directly, and as a matter of personal favour, to communicate their collective or individual opinions on any question of general law; nor, I should apprehend, can there be anything in the constitution of that most honourable court or the office of its judges to prevent them from acceding to such a request if it could be done without prejudice to their regular duties. It would be still easier for the Privy Council, a body whose ancient powers have never grown old, and whose functions have never ceased to be expansive and elastic, to seek the like assistance. And if the thing could be done at all, I suppose it could be done reciprocally from this side with no greater trouble. Such a proceeding could not, in any event, be common. It might happen twice or thrice in a generation, in a great and dubious case touching fundamental principles, like that of *Dalton* v. *Angus* (*a*)—a case in which some strong American opinions,

(*a*) 6 App. Ca. 740. Here an unanimous decision was arrived at; but it cannot be said that there was unanimity, or any decisive result, as to the reasons.

if they could have been obtained, would have been specially valuable and instructive.

Could the precedent be made once or twice in an informal and semi-official manner, it might safely be left to posterity to devise the means of turning a laudable occasional usage into a custom clothed with adequate form. As for the difficulties, they are of the kind that can be made to look formidable by persons unwilling to move, and can be made to vanish by active good will. Objections on the score of distance and delay would be inconsiderable, not to say frivolous. From Westminster to Washington is for our mails and despatches hardly so much of a journey as it was a century ago from Westminster to an English judge on the Northern or Western circuit. Opinions from every supreme appellate court in every English-speaking jurisdiction might now be collected within the time that Lord Eldon commonly devoted to the preliminary consideration of an appeal from the Master of the Rolls. At this day there is no mechanical obstacle in the way of judgments being rendered which should represent the best legal mind, not of this or that portion of the domains that acknowledge the Common Law, but of the whole. There is no reason why we should not live in hope of our system of judicial law being confirmed and exalted in a judgment-seat more than national, in a tribunal more comprehensive, more authoritative, and more august than any the world has yet known.

Some one may ask whether we look to see these things ourselves, or hope for them in our children's time. I cannot tell; the movement of ideas will not be measured beforehand in days or years. Our children and grandchildren may have to abide its coming, or it may come suddenly when we are least hopeful. Dreams are not versed in issuable matter, and have no dates. Only I feel that this one looks forward, and will be seen as waking light some day. If any one, being of little faith or over-curious, must needs ask in what day, I can answer only in the same fashion. We may know the signs though we know not when they will come. These things will be when we look back on our dissensions in the past as brethren grown up to man's estate and dwelling in unity look back upon the bickerings of the nursery and the jealousies of the class-room; when there is no use for the word "foreigner" between Cape Wrath and the Rio Grande, and the federated navies of the English-speaking nations keep the peace of the ocean under the Northern lights and under the Southern Cross, from Vancouver to Sydney and from the Channel to the Gulf of Mexico; when an indestructible union of even wider grasp and higher potency than the federal bond of these States has knit our descendants into an invincible and indestructible concord. For that day is coming too, and every one of us can do something, more or less, to hasten it; of us, I say, not only as citizens, but as especially bound thereto by the history and traditions of our profession which belong to America no less than to England. If we may deem that the fathers and founders of our polity can still take heed of our desires and endeavours, if we may think of them as still with us in spirit, watching over us and peradventure helping us, then surely we may not doubt that in this work Alfred and Edward and Chatham are well pleased to be at one with Washington and Hamilton and Lincoln. Under the auspices of such a fellowship we, their distant followers, are called; in their names we go forward; it is their destiny that we shall fulfil, their glory that we shall accomplish.

This, and nothing less than this, I claim here, an Englishman among Americans, a grateful guest but no stranger, for the full and perfect vocation of our Common Law.

THE EXPANSION OF THE COMMON LAW.

I. The Foundations of Justice.

The jurisprudence of the Western world is divided, for all practical purposes, between Germanic and Romanic law. Not that there is any such thing as an actual system of law derived wholly from Germanic or wholly from Roman sources; but there is no system whose formal structure is not, in the main, built on the one or the other of these foundations; unless indeed we ought to consider the law very recently established by the Civil Code of the German Empire as making a new departure in modern national jurisprudence. We may be allowed, in any case, to speak in the present tense, for historical purposes, of things as they were down to the close of the nineteenth century. Subject to this caution, it is generally true that the Continental nations of Western and Central Europe and the inhabitants of the colonies settled by them live under forms which, however modified by custom and recast in the codes of a more scientific age, are still those of Roman law. The Scandinavian lands are the only clear exception. Scandinavian law goes with the Germanic group; so does the isolated and very interesting system of Scottish law, notwithstanding that it put on a Roman face by a reception of Roman law and terminology, which is now known to have been late and superficial. The principal member of this group is, I need hardly say, the Common Law; the law of England carried around the world by English settlers, and now prevailing (with local modifications but with the same general principles) throughout the English-speaking parts of the British Empire beyond seas, the whole of the United States, except, I believe, one jurisdiction, and to a considerable extent, though partially and indirectly, in British India.

This, our law, is now a system capable of dealing with the most complex interests of modern affairs, and disposing of a variety of remedies adapted to different needs. It is alike ready to administer property in a friendly suit and to determine the disputes of rivals in trade; it will regulate the bounty of a charitable founder no less than it will punish crime. We call upon it to collect undisputed debts, and to grapple with the problems of high policy and public economy that are involved in commercial combinations. No development of business or science comes amiss to it. As commerce extends its operations and instruments, so does the law widen its conceptions. It learns from the masters of all crafts, and pays them with an ordered and secure life. If we inquire of its antiquity, we find that it has a continuous history of more than a thousand years. The Roman law, certainly, is older, some of it very much older. But the descent of the modern Civil Law of Europe from the Corpus Juris does not run smoothly. There are breaks and catastrophes. There are times of legal and of political anarchy, times when the Roman imperial law has to live, as it were, in hiding. The scientific study of it had to be laboriously revived in Western Europe, and to prepare the way for its reception as not merely a store of wisdom, but a rule claiming formal obedience; and that preparation was longer and harder, and the results less complete and universal, than we formerly supposed. The Common Law has not known any such interruptions. Political revolutions have fulfilled rather than destroyed its work; no tyrant or pretender has dared openly to lay hands on it. In the years when no man knew certainly whether Henry VI. or Edward IV. was king, judges might be removed and restored, but the king's law still held its certain place at Westminster; in the later time when there was no king at all in England, the course of justice was unaltered, except in formal style and titles. After the Restoration the statutes of the Commonwealth were treated as nullities, but no lawyer has ever attempted to discredit a judicial precedent of that period merely on account of its date. The fact is so notorious that, if I vouch Wallace on the Reporters for the particular proof of it, I do so chiefly for the pleasure of vouching so learned and distinguished an American author.

Neither has there been at any time any wholesale revolution in our judicial methods. The history of our courts is continuous for more than seven centuries. Edward I.'s judges, though fully aware that they were improving both law and procedure, certainly did not suppose that they were starting a new system of law different from that of Henry III. or Henry II., and certainly there is a sense in which we can now say that the law of King Edward VII., or of the State of Connecticut, is the same as the law of King Edward I. But there is also a sense in which it is paradoxical. An English or American practical lawyer of this day who adventures himself without special training among the documents of twelfth-century Anglo-Norman law, not to speak of any earlier generation, will find himself in a wild and strange land indeed (*a*). He will, in the first place, have very great difficulty in so much as making out what sort of world it is. He will meet with a crowd of strange terms and miss almost every familiar one. He will hear very little of a judge, nothing of a jury, nothing of professional advocates. In vain will he look for any recognition of what we now think elementary conditions of administering justice. No sign will appear of any rational or approximately rational process for deciding on disputed matters of fact. Oaths are counted, not weighed; the persons who swear are not witnesses; there is no evidence at all, in our sense, unless when a deed is produced. The court of the hundred or the county will seem more like a rather disorderly public meeting than a court of justice. Our modern observer may be apt to think that for a long time before and some time after the Norman Conquest our ancestors occupied such leisure as they had in cattle stealing by night and manslaughter and perjury in varying proportions by day; and as to some parts of the country he would not be very far wrong. He will certainly think that their justice was always crude, often barbarous, and very commonly inefficient. Nevertheless it is true that our modern Common Law has grown or been fashioned, or (lest we dispute prematurely about the right word) has in some way come out of these rudiments, unpromising as they are at first sight. For it is there,

(*a*) See the Appendix, for a short account of English law before the Norman Conquest.

and it has come there without any assignable break. From the beginning of the thirteenth to the middle of the nineteenth century there is no measure in the whole history of our legal system so revolutionary in form as the Judicature Acts in England or the introduction of "code pleading" in New York and other American states. The sheriff was with us before the Norman Conquest; he is with us still, and better known even among lawyers by his old English name than in the Latin disguise of *vice-comes;* his judicial functions, preserved or enlarged in Scotland, have disappeared in England, but he is still the chief executive officer of the law; he still performs his duties in person in America, though not in England except for ceremonial purposes; and I understand that in some American jurisdictions, where unsettled conditions have produced a certain reversion to the simplicity of our ancestors, the performance may still require a good deal of courage and activity. Criminal procedure has been changed, one may say, out of all knowledge since the thirteenth century; the Grand Jury is so much overshadowed by the later development of the petit jury that its functions might almost be neglected in giving a first general view of the present system to a layman or a foreigner; but in itself the Grand Jury is still very much what the Assize of Clarendon made it.

How shall we account for this combination of diversity with continuity, or where shall we find a likeness for it? Are we to think of the familiar gun that was repaired by being fitted with a new stock, a new lock and a new barrel, or the knife that a man kept forty years, giving it sometimes a new haft and sometimes a new blade? Or of an old house that has never been pulled down, but has been so much enlarged and altered by successive tenants, minded to improve it each for his own purposes, that hardly one room in it remains just as it was built? Or may we perchance discover, underlying all the confusion of detail, a real organic energy of growth, a "competence to be" and not only to be but to conquer?

We said that an Anglo-Saxon or Anglo-Norman county court would probably seem to us, if we could see it, rather like an ill-managed public meeting. But perhaps the sheriff or one of the notables—the persons whom Bracton calls by the mysterious name of *buzones*—if he could be brought to see us and hear our comments, might have a word to put in. He might say: "Doubtless you are wiser than we were, as after so many generations you ought to be. Doubtless we were unlearned folk, and our justice was rough. A public meeting, if you like. But is it nothing that we did keep it public? Had we not some root of the matter there? See what your modern books say, and then consider your judgment on our barbarism." Looking into our books, we find that in the year 1829 (that is to say, in the time of high Tory reaction following upon the French Revolution and the Napoleonic wars) certain justices of Lincolnshire turned one Daubney out of their justice-room when he offered to appear as attorney for a defendant charged with unlawfully keeping a gun to kill game. Daubney sued the justices for assault, and had a verdict for nominal damages, and the question whether he ought to have been non-suited came before the Court of King's Bench. The case was argued on the point whether the party was entitled to appear by attorney on a summons at petty sessions. But the court decided it on the ground that, the proceedings being judicial, the plaintiff, whether entitled to be there as attorney or not, was entitled as one of the public. The justices might not be bound to hear him; they had no right to remove him if there was room for him in the place where they were sitting and he behaved himself decently. For petty sessions are a court of justice, and "it is one of the essential qualities of a court of justice that its proceedings should be public" (*a*). The jurisdiction and powers of justices of the peace are, I need hardly say, derived wholly from statutes; and Parliament has been sometimes more and sometimes less imbued with the spirit of the Common Law. When this judgment was given, some of the duties of justices under Tudor statutes were very distinctly of an executive rather than a judicial kind; and in fact, under the Restoration, if not later, their investigation of crime included, together with the work of a public prosecutor, much that we should now think appropriate to a police officer. But when we pass from the second to the third quarter of the nineteenth century, we find that the Parliament of Queen Victoria has taken a widely different course from the Parliament of King Philip and Queen Mary. The secret inquisitorial proceeding has become open and judicial; there is no longer an examination of the prisoner, but a preliminary trial in court, the police-court, which in modern times is to many citizens the only visible and understood symbol of law and justice. The magistrate's office is more public than ever; the feeling that judgment should be done in the light of day has been strong enough to reassert itself after a partial eclipse. No such feeling exists in Continental Europe, or none of comparable strength. Here we have one tradition, at any rate,

(*a*) *Daubney* v. *Cooper*, 10 B. & C. 237, 240; 34 R. R. at p. 380.

which has persisted through all changes. Like other rules of practice, the rule of publicity is not quite inflexible; some few exceptions are allowed on grounds of decency or policy, and in some jurisdictions they have been confirmed or extended by statute. But as to these exceptions, reasonable as they are, it is significant that most of them are derived from the essentially Roman and canonical procedure of the spiritual courts. The settled judgment of our ancestors and ourselves is that publicity in the administration of the law is on the whole—to borrow words used by my friend Mr. Justice O. W. Holmes in another context—worth more to society than it costs. It may be worth while to observe that the publicity of the court itself is one thing and the indiscriminate publication of reports is another; the distinction is rather easy to forget.

Another point of Germanic procedure must seem very strange to learned persons bred in the civilian tradition; and, so far as we can tell, it is immemorial. *Nunquam aliter viderunt esse*, as the jurors of a medieval inquest might say. Namely, the parties before the court are wholly answerable for the conduct of their own cases. Litigation is a game in which the court is umpire. The rules are in the knowledge of the court and will be declared and applied by it as required. It is for the parties to learn the rules and play the game correctly at their peril. The court will not tell the plaintiff what step he ought to take next, neither will it tell the defendant whether the plaintiff has made a slip of which he can take advantage. The umpire will speak when his judgment is demanded; it is not his business if the players throw away chances. Perhaps the analogy of field manœuvres is even more appropriate. The Red commander may push forward an unsupported battery into a crushing fire at short range from Blue's unbroken infantry. Nobody will stop him; he will learn his mistake when his guns are put out of action. So it was in the ancient hundred and county courts, and so it was in the king's courts that supplanted them. Such is, in substance, the rule of our law to this very day. The battles of pleaders which were fought before our lady the Common Law at Westminster for six centuries were true to an older tradition, and the tradition is still alive under all tho changes of outward form. "The rule that the court is not to dictate to parties how they should frame their case is one that ought always to be preserved. But that rule is, of course, subject to this modification and limitation, that the parties must not offend against the rules of pleading which have been laid down by the law" (*a*). Even those rules are not generally enforced by the court, except on the application of a party. Pleaders may let a cause go to issue on demurrable pleadings if they choose, and there are, or under the old practice were, many reasons that might make such a choice prudent.

This neutral or expectant attitude of the court is significant for the substance as well as the practice of the law. It is as unsafe as ever it was to rely on the supposed authority of a case for a point not expressly discussed and passed upon, but supposed to be implied in the decision. "The attention of the court was not called to that point"; many a plausible argument has been checked by that answer, always legitimate and sometimes complete. Another branch of the same principle is that, according to the immemorial custom of Germanic procedure, the court will have

(*a*) *Per* Bowen, L. J., in *Knowles* v. *Roberts* (1888), 38 Ch. Div. 263, 270.

nothing to do with making inquiries to find out things for itself. It is not there to inquire, or to do anything of its own motion, but to hear and determine between parties according to the proofs which the parties can bring forward. Some things, undoubtedly, are notorious. The suitors of the county or the hundred are men of common sense as well as doomsmen; they cannot help knowing what all the neighbours know. The rules of judicial notice in our modern doctrine of evidence are only the scientific refinement of broad and popular postulates. But outside the bounds of manifest public knowledge, the court knows nothing but what is properly set before it by the parties, and, except for quite recent statutory powers which in England are not much used, has no means of informing itself.

It is not so easy to give a short name to the principle now under consideration as to the rule of publicity which we mentioned first. We may call it, perhaps, the rule of neutrality. Nothing in our procedure is more characteristic, more settled, or more continuous. Any apparent exceptions to it in our earlier records may be explained by the special circumstances. Either the proceeding was not really judicial, or there was something abnormal about the jurisdiction, or the court was acting on proof on which the parties had put themselves beforehand. It is easy, in these and other ways, to misunderstand the facts of archaic procedure if one has not grasped the principles. Thus we have a record from the time of King Cnut, in the first half of the eleventh century, where the Herefordshire county court sent three of its members to speak with a certain lady against whom her son claimed land under some alleged grant or covenant made by her. It looks at first sight as if the court had sent a commission to take evidence for its own use. But it is really quite otherwise. The lady is represented in court by one Thurkil White; apparently he is the nearest male kinsman in right of his wife; but he says he does not know the case. Accordingly three thanes, who are named, and who doubtless were chosen as discreet and impartial persons, are forthwith deputed to see the lady, for she lives within an easy ride. They ask her what she has to say, and she emphatically repudiates her son's claim and declares that Thurkil's wife (who is present with her) is to succeed to everything. "Here sits Leoflæd, my kinswoman, whom I grant both my land and my gold, both raiment and garment, and all that I own, after my day." She bids them "do thanelike and well" by declaring her mind to the shire-moot and taking all its good men to witness. Practically the court is in this manner fully informed; but it has not assumed jurisdiction to administer interrogatories. Thurkil said he had no instructions, and therefore could not tell what to say. The court, for greater certainty, sends trusted members of its own body to take the instructions; there is as yet no such office as that of an attorney or counsel, much less any notion of communications with one's adviser being confidential. Obviously the lady was not only willing but eager to speak out, and there is no question of any one having authority to require it of her. When the thanes return to the court (which presumably had been disposing of other business meanwhile) they repeat the lady's declaration; but the court does not offer to do anything. It is for Thurkil to take up the cause, and now he knows what to do. "Then Thurkil White stood up in the gemot and asked all the thanes to give his wife clear the lands that her kinswoman granted her, and they did so." Whereupon Thurkil (the court having no written record of its own) prudently rides off to the nearest considerable church and gets a learned clerk to set down the whole matter in the blank leaves of a Gospel book. All that properly concerns us here is to see that the court does not act *ex officio*, notwithstanding first appearances. But we may as well sum up the formal aspect of the case to make the explanation complete. The plaintiff states a claim; it does not appear how he expected to make it good; but when it becomes known that there is a substantial defence, he is unable to bring any proof, and is not in a position to tender his own oath or require the defendant's. In fact he has nothing to say, and abandons the suit. Incidentally the defendant's kinsman has brought before the court the defendant's own declaration and her request that the court will bear witness to it; and this is granted without demur. I confess I do not know whether the action of the thanes is strictly a doom of the county court or only a solemn witnessing of the lady's deposition by its members; but I do not think any one would have appreciated the distinction at the time. Of the lady's title to the land and power to dispose of it we are told nothing; Anglo-Saxon records are commonly inartificial in such matters; but the omission may be technically justified, for there is evidently no dispute on that score. Almost certainly the land was book-land, and the disposition—which was rather a deferred or "post-obit" grant than a will—was within the powers conferred by the terms of the book (*a*). One cannot help surmising that the thanes of Herefordshire knew a good deal about the parties

(*a*) Cod. Dipl. DCCLV. Essays in Anglo-Saxon Law, p. 365.

and their character, and it is curious that the lady's name is not given. Perhaps she was a very great personage.

We have, again, in the *Textus Roffensis* (*a*), an account of the great county court held at Penenden Heath in 1072, where Lanfranc recovered divers lands of the see of Canterbury against Odo, and procured a comprehensive declaration of its franchises. This was only a few years after the Conquest, and the procedure is obviously the old English procedure; the story is fairly plain, but not without pitfalls for the unwary. King William, on Lanfranc's complaint, ordered a special county court to be held: all the men of the county, and of adjacent counties too, both French and English, and in particular Englishmen skilled in the ancient laws and customs, were to meet. A little farther on we read the names of eminent persons who attended, including "Æthelric, Bishop of Chichester, a very old man and most learned in the laws of the land, who was brought there in a wagon (*in una quadriga*) by the king's command, to discuss and explain the ancient legal customs." A modern reader unversed in archaic law might begin to think of special jurymen, expert witnesses and assessors. Indeed, it would not be very surprising if, on so great an occasion, the king, who held the court by the Bishop of Coutances as his deputy, and knew from his experience as Duke of Normandy what an inquest was, had used exceptional methods. But it is quite clear that all the persons mentioned were members of the court and nothing else, though members whose age and experience gave special weight to their counsels. Even the venerable Bishop of Chichester, who received (as I read the somewhat ambig-

(*a*) Essays in Anglo-Saxon Law, p. 369; Bigelow, Plac. Anglo-Normann. 4.

uous text) the unique honour of the king sending a cart for him, was in form only one doomsman among a multitude of equal fellow-doomsmen. It does not appear definitely how the customs claimed by Lanfranc were stated to the court, but the case seems to have been conducted by Lanfranc himself. Nor does it appear whether Odo made any and what kind of defence. It is remarkable that the declaration of the court, as reported, is much against the interest of the Crown, but the king does not seem to have made any difficulty. The point now before us, however, is simply that there is not any trace of inquisitorial procedure (*a*). If there is anything in modern practice at all like King William's very just and reasonable precautions on this occasion, it may perhaps be found in the manner of making up the Judicial Committee of the Privy Council for a particular sitting, according as the appeals to be heard are from ecclesiastical courts, or from English-speaking colonies under the Common Law, or from India.

So far we have assumed that there is a litigation between parties, a matter of what we now call civil business. I need not remind you that, in archaic judicature, the distinction between public and private law, though we cannot say it is wholly ignored, is rudimentary. We need not, therefore, be surprised if the part of the State is wanting, or at any rate weak and vague, in Anglo-Saxon and Anglo-Norman criminal justice. The popular court has as little to do with official inquiry in a case of theft or man-

(*a*) Notwithstanding the opinion of some modern writers (in one case afterwards withdrawn), I can find nothing of the kind either in the Textus Roffensis or in Eadmer. Indeed, Eadmer's words, "Ex communi omnium astipulatione et iudicio," seem to imply the contrary.

slaying as on a claim of title. It is merely the executor of the law on proof made in due form by oath or ordeal, or else on its own witness of manifest and undeniable facts, as where the slayer is taken red-handed, or the thief with the stolen goods. But when we come to the conscious and deliberate establishment of the king's justice, we might well expect such rulers as Henry II. and Edward I. to disregard the popular tradition and strike out some independent line; to take up a position of official and paternal authority, doing what seems best in their eyes for the general welfare and informing themselves by any means they think fit, and for that purpose to introduce some kind of official procedure. For such a procedure the resources of the Canon Law could have easily supplied a model. There was no need, however, to go to the Canon Law. The king had, if he had chosen to see it in that light, a readier instrument in his own hand, ultimately of Roman origin but imported by the Conqueror as part of the Frankish administrative machinery which the Roman Court had adopted. This was the sworn inquest, a special and royal form of procedure with nothing popular about it in the first instance. Directly or through instructions to the sheriff, the king could appoint commissioners of inquiry on any system he chose, or on no system at all. Their finding on oath was only a report; it had nothing in common with the dooms of the popular courts; the king or his deputy had all the active control of the matter. There was no formal reason why the jurors should either inquire or report in public. It was not even obvious that they need always inquire at all, for the one point of practice which became fixed earliest was that they were chosen from the persons presumed to be best acquainted with the facts.

Here, one would think, was ample material for a royal judicial system of a masterful inquisitorial type, overriding all the archaic popular traditions, and concentrating real power, as regards matters of criminal jurisdiction reserved to the king, in the hands of expert officials; and we know that the reserved cases, if we may convert that ecclesiastical term to a secular sense, tended to include, and in time did include, all serious offences. If we could now cut ourselves off from our knowledge of what actually came to pass later, we might well consider the most plausible inference from the state of English justice under Henry II. to be that the popular element was doomed, and that, if it had any hope of successful development elsewhere, it must be in some country where the king's authority was much weaker. Any such forecast would, in fact, have been wholly wrong.

The personal designs and ambitions of the Angevin kings looked in quite other directions; and, although they certainly neither intended nor expected the jury to become a bulwark of popular liberty and the strongest protection against any attempt to tamper with the principle of publicity, they did not intend the contrary. It never occurred to them to make use of the procedure by inquest, while its forms were still plastic, as a tool of absolutist policy. They considered the inquest merely as a useful working method of enlarging the king's jurisdiction and bringing well-earned profit in fines and otherwise to the king's exchequer, and the best way of promoting those ends was to develop the institution, or let it develop itself, along the lines of least resistance. Thus the popular instinct was left free to do its work out of sight and without raising alarm; and it found its firmest leverage just where the new procedure, in its earlier shape, might have been thought least democratic and most capable of serving, we will not say arbitrary power, but a system of official and paternal administration. Jurors are a set of men—twelve or some other number, that was a variable matter of detail to begin with—sworn and charged to report on certain facts presumed to be within their knowledge. Neighbours to the scene are therefore wanted. For getting at such men the ancient local divisions, hundred and township, are ready to hand, with their rough, but fairly sufficient, organization. So the new Frankish and Norman inquest was wedded, from the time of the Domesday survey onwards, to the old customs of the land; and the issue was more English than the English themselves had been. The jurors, grand or petty, were not mere official nominees; they were made representative that they might be satisfactory witnesses; but, once being representative, they carried a weight beyond that of mere witness; they stood for the judgment of the people, and became a social and political power. Later the judges, not only in the interest of the Crown, but to secure uniform administration of justice, found it necessary to give precise instructions to juries as to the questions of fact which were open to them, and lay down rules as to the testimony that might be received. This process did indeed set limits to the discretion of juries, but it confirmed their power and importance within the settled limits, and increased the dignity of their office. Verdicts took over the solemnity, one may fairly call it the sanctity, that had attached to the old popular judgments. All the conditions, even those which at first sight were unfavorable, worked together for the continuance of the original Germanic ideals under more apt and efficient forms.

Moreover, to return to the point immediately before us, the concurrent application of the jury process to civil and criminal business tended to assimilate prosecutions at the suit of the Crown to litigation between individuals; and from the thirteenth century onwards the institution of justices of assize worked potently to the same end. The judge acting as a commissioner of gaol delivery could not dismiss from his mind the lessons which he had learned as an advocate, which his companion justice was putting in practice in the adjoining court as a commissioner of *nisi prius*, and which he might himself have to put in practice in that capacity at the next term on the circuit. Slowly and fitfully, but in the long run surely, these constant forces produced their effect. More and more the king came to be regarded in his own court, not as the supreme head of national justice exhibiting and punishing the crimes which his officers had discovered, but as a party, though an exceptional and privileged party, bound to make his cause good. He was not an examining magistrate, but a plaintiff suing the prisoner before the judge and jury. The rule that a plaintiff must prove his case was applied to the king and his ministers, all the more effectively because it was taken as a matter of course, and not made a subject of panegyric; and when the political controversies of the seventeenth century brought its importance into light, it was too late to go back upon it. Encroachments and attempted encroachments of extraordinary on ordinary jurisdiction were indeed not wanting; some of them came very near success. We shall have to consider these later. In this place I have only to point out, resisting the temptation of details, that they all ultimately failed. The ideals of the Common Law triumphed, and the rule that the burden of proof is on the plaintiff was carried over from the civil to the criminal side of judicature. It has long since become familiar in all men's mouths as the presumption of the prisoner's innocence; a venerable and still useful if not perfectly accurate phrase. Not that the result is arrived at by a strictly logical course. Our modern maxim quietly relegates the grand jury and its office to a position little better than ornamental. An intelligent layman reading the common form of indictment with a fresh mind will have some difficulty in seeing why a man whom the body of the county has explicitly charged, on the oath of its lawful men, with such and such a crime, should claim the benefit of any presumption. As Sir James Stephen has said, "Why should a man be presumed to be innocent when at least twelve men have positively sworn to his guilt?" From the medieval point of view he would be right enough. A man solemnly accused by the witness of his countrymen is more than half guilty, and our ancestors dealt with him accordingly. But the working of deep-seated national instinct is not bound to logic. It comes up to the light where best it can and acts on such material as it finds to hand. At present the assimilation of which we spoke is all but complete. The king or the commonwealth, on the prosecution of the Attorney-General or Nokes, as the case may be, sues John Stiles, and the general lines of a trial for felony differ little (in some jurisdictions, for aught I know, they may not differ at all) from those of an action for the price of goods sold and delivered. In some respects, indeed, there are differences in favor of the prisoner; and, so far as the grand jury has any effectual function at the present day, it is that of stopping frivolous or otherwise unsustainable prosecutions at an early stage. We have now, in most common-law jurisdictions, completed the analogy of criminal to civil proceedings by allowing the prisoner to be a witness on his own behalf. In England the change was strenuously opposed by some persons of great ability and experience, but is believed to be well justified by the results.

Yet another point is to be observed about our ancient county court. The law which is administered there is strange enough to modern eyes, but still it is some kind of law, and the court must have some means of ascertaining it. Where does the court find its law? Does it follow the letter of some sacred writing? Does it take the rules from a king, or a priesthood, or any body of persons having any sort of official authority? Where technical and official designations are still so vague and in an early stage of formation, it is not very easy to put our question in any terms wholly free from anachronism. But in substance this is a real question admitting of a real answer, and, whatever may be the least incorrect form of expressing either in modern language, the substance of the answers is in the negative. The court has no external authority to look to. For every case it must find its own law, for there is no other than that which is declared to be law by the court. Indeed, the law of the land may be said to live in the witness of the county and the hundred. It is not clear that there was any other authority even for the text of the dooms issued from time to time by the king and his wise men for the purpose of consolidating, amending, or supplementing the customary rules. The suitors of the court had to take on themselves the burden of knowing the law as well as of applying it. The king and the Witan can to some extent make law, though it certainly was not supposed in the twelfth or thirteenth century that the king, with or without his council, had anything like the unlimited legislative power which our modern constitution ascribes to the king in Parliament; in any case only the court can interpret the law they have made. In other words, interpretation is a strictly judicial function with which neither the executive nor the legislative power has anything to do. This is as ancient as any tradition of the Common Law, and it is still in full force on both sides of the Atlantic. Not that the suitors of the old popular courts need be presumed to have given their dooms capriciously or without advice. It is true that we do not find any one officially entitled to instruct them; for the sheriff summons the court and presides, but has no voice in giving judgment. There does not appear in our documents any definable person wielding such an authority as in Iceland, in a corresponding stage of the closely allied Scandinavian institutions, was attributed to the "Speaker of the Law"; nor am I prepared without evidence to postulate his existence. Yet we need not doubt that there was always some man, or a small group of men, whose opinion about a disputed point of custom did in fact carry great weight. It is indeed a matter of human nature rather than of positive institution that in every assembly whose whole number is not very small there will be a few members more capable or more active than the rest who, in Bacon's phrase, sway all the business. The legal independence of the doomsmen in the county and the hundred court is, however, what now concerns us; and it is well attested. Only in the case of divided opinion, it seems, the sheriff, as the king's executive officer, had a discretion to act on the opinion of the majority or wait for the judgment of another court (*a*). But the courts of the

(*a*) P. & M. Hist. Eng. Law, i. 552-3.

hundred and the county are, as we all know, long since extinct. How then has their custom survived?

As time went on the popular courts faded into insignificance, then into oblivion; the name and functions of the ancient doomsmen vanished, and the law was delivered in the king's courts by the king's justices. We have already said that an impartial observer in the thirteenth century might well have expected the jury to become a strictly official piece of machinery. Not less might he have expected the king's judges to regard themselves and to be regarded as mere exponents of the king's will, and to prefer the interests of the Crown to all other considerations. But it fell out quite otherwise. Professional tradition and public spirit were too strong for royal influence. As early as the thirteenth century the judges were the servants of the law first and the king afterwards. Opinions might plausibly differ, before the Revolution of 1688, as to the amount of power which the law conferred on the king; but even in the worst of times only the weakest and the worst of lawyers could be found to give any countenance to the extreme royalist pretensions that would fain have set the king above the law.

Certainly the power of the king's judges, a compact body of learned persons directly representing the king's authority, was very great. Their office was, and is, deliberately exalted. To this day justices of assize take precedence, while they are on their circuit, of all other persons in the county (*a*). No less certainly the judicial

(*a*) The sheriff, who is otherwise the first person in the county, though it is not quite settled whether he comes before the lord-lieutenant, has a writ of assistance directed to all archbishops, bishops, &c. The commissioners of assize are accompanied by a like writ power was used with great freedom to repress diversity of local customs and establish uniform rules as far as the jurisdiction of the king's courts extended. But the courts were really doing the work of the ancient tradition, inasmuch as the uniformity which they established was not according to the king's pleasure, but according to law, and was far more capable of resisting executive interference than the customs which it superseded. If rival provincial customs had been allowed to take defined form, they might have invited an overruling despot. The Custom of the Realm was another matter.

In countries where judgment and justice were local and multiple, every development of rules within this and that limited sphere might seem obnoxious to the central authority as tending to paternalism. In England the guardians of custom which was not particular but general were intimately connected with the central authority itself, and the sanctity of customary law was indistinguishable from that of all institutions and dignities, royal and others. The king's own power had nothing better to rest on, for we are speaking of times long before the speculative doctrine of divine right was invented.

A further development, already foreseen in the thirteenth century and settled beyond questioning in the fifteenth, is that which gives our jurisprudence its most peculiar and striking character. Judicial interpretation of the law is the only authentic interpretation. So far as the particular case is concerned this may seem an obvious

directed to the sheriff himself. Not that a commissioner of assize need be a judge; but the working commissioners have always been, as a rule, judges of the superior courts, and their special dignity is for all practical purposes merged in that of the judicial office.

matter. Positively, the court is there for the purpose of deciding, and has to arrive at a decision. Negatively, no other authority has any right to interfere with a court of justice acting within its competence; this is perhaps not quite so obvious, but may be supposed to be the rule in all or very nearly all civilized jurisdictions. But the Common Law goes much beyond this immediate respect for judicial authority. The judgment looks forward as well as backward. It not only ends the strife of the parties but lays down the law for similar cases in the future. The opinion of a Superior Court embodied in the reasons of its judgment stands, with us, on a wholly different footing from any other form of learned opinion. I am not aware that any historical reason can be given for this other than the early consolidation of royal jurisdiction in England, and the administration of justice by the king's judges on a uniform system throughout the country. Probably we shall never know how much they simplified, or whether their methods were always what we should now call strictly judicial. But we know that in the time of Henry I. it was still possible to talk of district bodies of custom as existing in Wessex, in Mercia, and in the Danelaw; that in the time of Henry II. there were still undefined varieties of usage, which may or may not have been confined to procedure and to the rules of inheritance; and that in the time of Henry III. men spoke only of the laws and customs of England, and whatever did not conform to the Common Law as declared by the king's court had to justify itself as an exception on some special ground. The king's judges, and they alone, had power to lay down what the general custom of England, in other words the Common Law, for the terms are synonymous in our books, must be taken to be. Quite possibly their own views of convenience counted for something in the process of determination; at the same time it is certain that, so far as universal or very general usage really existed, the king's judges, doing the king's business in all parts of the country and comparing their experience at Westminster, were the persons best qualified to know it. The law of the thirteenth century was judge-made law in a fuller and more literal sense than the law of any succeeding century has been. Laymen sometimes talk of judge-made law as if judges were legislators and could lay down any rule they chose. It is needless to explain to a legal audience that this is not so. Judges are indeed bound to find some rule for deciding every case that comes before them, but they must do it without contradicting established principles, and in conformity with the reasons on which previous decisions were founded. They may supplement and enlarge the law as they find it, or rather they must do so from time to time, as the novelty of questions coming before them may require; but they must not reverse what has been settled. Only express legislation can do that. But even now there are a certain number of cases "of the first impression." In the thirteenth century their number was large.

Henry III.'s and Edward I.'s judges did not rejoice in, or groan under, a library of printed reports; they had many new cases and little recorded authority, and were almost compelled to be original. But they certainly intended to be consistent, and were aware that their judgments were regarded as fixing the law. One reason why judicial precedents acquired exclusive authority was the absence of any other source of law capable of competing with them. Legislation was still exceptional and occasional, and there was no independent learned class. When the king's court began to keep its rolls in due course, the rolls themselves were the only evidence of the principles by which the court was guided; and the earliest treatises on the Common Law were produced by members of the judicial staff, or under their direction. It is also to be considered that the king's courts, as their functions became defined, had to regulate their own procedure if there was to be any order at all in their business; and that, in a state of government where both law and procedure are new, it is hard to draw an exact line between them, or to provide for urgent matters of procedure without determining the bent of the law itself. Sir Henry Maine's observations on the dominant importance of procedure in archaic law may now be called classical, and are presumed to be familiar to all historical students.

Thus the king's courts were driven, in more than one way, to be self-sufficient. Willing or not, they would still have had to make their own practice, and in doing so they could not help making a good deal of law. Not that we have any reason to look on the judges of the thirteenth and fourteenth centuries as persons unwilling to rise to the height of great responsibilities. Some of them were wiser and more valiant than others. We may see in Bracton opinions which, if they had prevailed, would have taken away grave reproach from the law, but which did not prevail because they were too bold for their day. But on the whole, the makers of English law and polity in the critical period of construction were not lacking in either wisdom or valour.

Another consequence of the greatest moment for public law and liberty followed from the exercise of a single and supreme judicial power at the king's judgment-seat and in his name. There was no question of setting up immunities or privileged law for the king's servants, no claim that acts of State should be above the law of the land. Who should judge the king's servants if not the king's own judges? True, there were diversities of jurisdiction and procedure, of which we read with amused curiosity in Blackstone; but the eagerness of every court to attract business to itself made short work of them, swamping them in fictions which were certainly beneficial, and, as they were too barefaced to deceive any one, may fairly be called innocent. It is true, again, that there came a time of high prerogative doctrine and extraordinary jurisdiction, when counsellors who were statesmen first and lawyers afterwards could exhort the king to make the judges know their places as "lions under the throne," and had plans for removing matters where the Crown was concerned from the ordinary courts (*a*). But then it was too late. The tradition of the Common Law was fixed, and all the pride of a distinguished and influential profession was enlisted in its support; and, what was more, the people had come to know and value it.

We come round, then, by ways at first sight devious and unlikely, to the affirmation and even strengthening of the ancient rules. Courts of justice are public; they judge between parties, and do not undertake an official inquiry, not even in criminal cases or in affairs of State; the court itself is the only authorized interpreter of the law which it administers; and there is no personal or official privilege against its jurisdiction.

(*a*) See Dicey, Law of the Constitution, 6th ed. 346—348; Bacon, Essay of Judicature.

These are the principles of which we find the rudiments in the earliest justice of our ancestors; which were maintained and developed through all political vicissitudes in English history, and crossed the Atlantic with the institutions and traditions of the mother country; and which still distinguish the administration of the law in every quarter of the world and every jurisdiction where the Common Law has taken root.

II. The Scales of Justice.

UNDER the rude and inadequate forms of the ancient popular courts we have been able to discern principles of lasting value, which are still at the very foundation of our judicial system and of our public law, and of which little is said on any common occasion, just because we accept them as matters of course. Now the popular courts were wholly incompetent to adapt themselves to a new state of society, and therefore, to maintain themselves and their traditions either for better or worse. Their constitution was essentially provincial, archaic and unprogressive. No system of national justice could ever come out of them; nor is there anything that strikes a student of our legal history more forcibly than the swiftness of their decline, after the thirteenth century, into insignificance and all but total oblivion (*a*). They were supplanted, as is notorious, for greater matters by the king's courts or the palatine courts which had unlimited legal franchises, and for smaller matters partly by the courts of private jurisdic-

(*a*) Their judicial functions appear to have been a vanishing quantity in the Elizabethan age. From an early time the king and his judges were teaching the sheriff and the county court to know their place. I quite agree with Mr. G. B. Adams (Amer. Hist. Rev. viii. 487) that Henry I.'s writ (Liebermann, *Quadrip.* p. 165) was not enabling but restrictive.

tions, enjoying immunities and exercising powers of every lower degree, and partly by the privileged jurisdictions of cities and boroughs. For the present purpose it is needless to dwell on the complicated, sometimes anomalous, and always interesting distinctions which are to be observed among these various authorities. Whatever might be their particular historical origin and legal warrant, the local courts agreed, in fact, with very few exceptions of any importance, in imitating the king's courts. The procedure and methods of the king's judges became the general model. So far did the Bishop of Durham carry the logic of his regalities that he found no difficulty in issuing, as temporal lord, prohibitions addressed to himself as bishop. It may be taken as a safe rule, throughout the formative period of the common law, that what the superior courts are doing to-day will be done by the inferior courts on some morrow not far off. Royal justice is the predominant and directing justice. The question now before us is how it became truly national, and preserved the substantial good points of ancient Germanic polity, while it discarded the obsolete forms.

Unless we fall back on the older mechanical theories which ignored the actions and reactions of human societies, and regarded institutions as plastic material in the hand of the lawgiver, the question is not at first sight easy. Not that the mechanical method would give us a plausible solution even on its own ground. Men called Edward I. the English Justinian; the comparison is at best superficial. A Justinian having no classical treatises of Papinian and Ulpian to make his Digest withal, no Gaius to revise for his Institutes, no golden age of the Antonines, no tradition of Labeo, no Twelve Tables, not so much as a

Theodosian Code (*a*), must be a strange thing for a civilian to imagine. But not even their aims were similar. Justinian consolidated and stereotyped the work of greater generations, whose development was already, for the time being, arrested. He worked in no prophetic spirit, but dreamed of finality. His service to the world was to provide a body in which the soul of Roman law, weary but not dead, might sleep until the appointed time for awaking. Very different was the soul for which Edward I. and his counsellors had to furnish an earthly tabernacle; a soul young and puissant, ardent with the fire and not yet freed from the rudeness of new life, setting forth on a mission of which she was all unconscious, whose extent no means of knowledge could then comprehend, and whose course no human wisdom could descry. And yet this much was clear to our founders of the thirteenth century, to William Raleigh and to Henry of Bratton no less than to Montfort, that they were giving the best of their lives to no common work.

But the very fact that the making of the custom of the realm was no common task, nor to be accomplished with common instruments, involved a grave danger, or so it seems to us looking back. The power that the king used was nothing arbitrary or new. It was, in principle, accepted from of old. But it was not ordinary judicial power; it was an extraordinary resource for extraordinary need, almost what we should now call an emergency power. A man might betake himself to the king if he

(*a*) I need hardly remind the learned reader that in the second half of the thirteenth century the text of the Anglo-Saxon dooms was as obsolete as it is now, and less understood. The vagaries of that puzzling work the Mirror of Justices, coupled with its failure to produce any effect, only confirm this.

failed to find justice in the popular courts, but only on that condition. So we learn from the Anglo-Saxon dooms. Let it be well observed that the failure must be total. It was not enough that the suitor was dissatisfied with a decision which had been given. He had no standing before the king unless he had tried in vain to get any decision at all, or the jurisdiction was usurped, or the judgment of the court was openly set at naught. The king had no jurisdiction to reverse the dooms of the county or the hundred on appeal. Archaic law knows nothing of any appeal, in our modern sense, from the judgment of a competent tribunal once possessed of the cause. It does take notice, more or less, of want of competence in the jurisdiction or procedure, and of wilful denial of right, and of inability to do right by reason of external hindrances, of which the chief is the overbearing power of great men strong enough to defy the court. If the king is called in, it is to break down a resistance hardly distinguishable from incipient rebellion; and indeed the name of the writ of rebellion carries on this point of view into the settled and peaceful practice of courts of equity (themselves a later development of extraordinary royal power) down to a time within living memory. We must think not of the everyday executive process of the sheriff's officer, but of a requisition for Federal troops, if we would realize the medieval beginnings of the king's justice. It was a special and higher justice, not conceived, at first, as meant for common occasions or common persons.

This kind of interference might well be expected to become, with the increasing strength of the monarchy, frequent, and from being frequent to become systematic.

But it does not appear obvious why rule and order thus brought in from above should have any continuity with earlier traditions. It would not have been hard, one would think, to seek elsewhere for guiding principles. We are apt to forget how modern is the compact insularity of Britain and British affairs. John had lost Normandy and Edward failed to win Scotland, but England under the first Edward after the Conquest was a Continental power of no mean rank. On the Continent Roman jurisprudence was in the pride of its revival; a new stream of foreign influence, more refined and more penetrating than the Norman, was making its way in England. There must have been much temptation for learned persons to regard any specially English ideas and usages as a kind of provincial heresy. Theologians, at any rate, could tell them of a British heresiarch. Or, if the matter was too stubborn, the attempt might have been made to force it into some mould of Romanist doctrine; Bracton did indeed make such an attempt on paper, though to a much less extent than has been supposed, and, I venture to think, neither expecting nor desiring much practical result. An imposing parade of learned reasons might have been mustered with ease in favour of innovation on a grand scale. Statecraft, scholarship, cosmopolitan liberality, were all ready to be enlisted. And yet Edward I. built on the old foundations and built firm. The building lasted till our own day; the foundations are unmoved. Shall we not say that he was a bold as well as a wise man? Daring greatly to be insular, we stood aloof from the Pandects and the Lex Regia; we made Parliament and the Year Books, and our seeming barbarism is justified round the world.

Far be it from me to say that Edward I. could really have done otherwise if he would. I believe in the divinity that shapes our ends. Rather the fact that our institutions were ordered as they were, and seemed to be so quite naturally, bears witness to the depth of national sense and tradition, a depth under a surface hardly ruffled by conscious effort. Probably no one, at the time, set himself to weigh reasons as in face of a large problem, or had any clear perception that he stood at a parting of the ways. We may think of reasons in detail, but they may be convincing only to a modern mind. Such a motive, for example, as jealousy of the Holy Roman Empire and its possible pretensions appears to lose much of its force when we remember not only that the Emperor was a long way off, and his ambitions looked beyond the Alps, but that an English king's son had been elected King of the Romans (*a*). For my own part, I am inclined to give thanks for a quality in our national character which has perhaps never been fully accounted for. We prefer to call it practical wisdom; an impartial philosopher might put it in a neutral category of moral inertia, while a censorious critic might vilipend it negatively as want of imagination, or positively as a ballast of stupidity. Sometimes it is a gift rather than a defect not to see too far or too wide at once; it may save us from fighting against the gods. Not otherwise did we rise to the height of our destinies in India; not otherwise have these States added a large unwritten chapter to their Constitution, a chapter still exceeding hard for the wisest to read. Our bent is

(*a*) The general interest in Richard of Cornwall's election is well illustrated by Bracton's examples of conditions, which tempt one to guess that there was a good deal of betting on the event.

not to think of ourselves as setting an example to the world, or prescribing rules to our remote posterity, but to take up the day's work, be it more or less, and handle it as best we may. With us it is not "What memorable thing can we achieve?" but "How shall we get this business through?" No way, certainly, is exempt from temptations and besetting risks, and this has its own. It may lose us great opportunities, or blind us to impending trouble. Overmuch acquiescence in it leads to narrowness, to niggardly dealing with great interests, to lack of resource in great occasions, to mishaps, misunderstandings, friction, and waste. But on the whole it is less likely to end in crushing disaster than the far-reaching ambition which lays out new worlds for itself, and thinks to build them by forcing the hand of Providence. The founders of the common law worked faithfully for what they could see, and were rewarded beyond all reach of vision. We cannot say they were altogether of English race; it is at least doubtful whether some of them could speak English, and not doubtful that many of them did not habitually speak it; but they were thoroughly imbued with the national character, and though they might speak French and write Latin, spoke and wrote as Englishmen.

We have already renounced any claim to give a complete explanation. One way or another, it was judged or felt that the king's regular jurisdiction would be acceptable and stable only so far as it respected the spirit of popular justice. Indications were not wanting; the Grand Assize had been hailed as a master-stroke of reform, but the inventiveness of the king's clerks in framing new writs was checked as a grievance. I do not know whether there was a sort of general suspicion that the king's officers meddled too much, or the lords of private courts were afraid of losing profitable business. Few students of our legal history will think that the restrictive injunction of the Provisions of Oxford was wise, or that the partial relaxation effected by the Statute of Westminster was adequate. Parliament would not let the courts frame new writs and was incompetent to frame them itself, and "the Common Law was dammed and forced to flow in unnatural, artificial channels" (*a*). But our business here is to understand the strength of the root, not to justify the growth of all its branches. Thus the king's courts, at the outset of their career, came under a rule which we shall find to run through the whole of our legal history, and never to be neglected with impunity. It may be expressed thus: extraordinary jurisdiction succeeds only by becoming ordinary. By this we mean not only that the judgment and remedies which were once matter of grace have to become matter of common right, but that right must be done according to the fundamental ideas of English justice of which we spoke in the first lecture. The Court of Chancery conformed in good time, and prospered; the Court of Star Chamber, warped to political ends, resisted and perished, involving one or two harmless victims in its fall.

In one capacity, indeed, the king was already, from the Conquest onwards, a judge with ordinary and original jurisdiction. It is an elementary rule of feudal tenure that every lord is bound to do justice to his tenants. The tenant's duty of doing suit to the lord's court is correlative to the lord's duty of holding it. One may read of this, perhaps, better in Beaumanoir than in English books,

(*a*) Maitland, Bracton's Note Book, i. 7.

but there is no doubt that the principle was accepted in England as much as in Normandy or Aquitaine (*a*). Now the king was the greatest of lords; confiscation, commendation, and the application of the theory of tenure to spiritual persons and houses of religion, had swelled a patrimony which was already considerable in the time of Edward the Confessor. The king's tenants naturally carried their disputes to him. In the Anglo-Norman period it is not always easy to see how far he is acting as judge, how far as a paternal arbitrator, and how far in the exercise of a supreme executive discretion. Sometimes we find him administering specific relief in ways not possible to a court with a fixed scheme of process and remedies (*b*). None the less these exigencies produced, on the whole, a habit of acting judicially, which in the course of the twelfth century ripened into a definite procedure. Henry II. seems to have enjoyed holding a formal court and discussing charters. The keener legal intellect of the thirteenth century could distinguish the king's seignorial justice from his public justice, as, on a greater scale, the framers of the *Statutum Walliae* distinguished with perfect accuracy between his feudal overlordship of Wales and the full political sovereignty acquired by conquest.

If the king was the greatest of lords, he was also the greatest of householders. From the earliest times he must have exercised a personal and domestic jurisdiction over his immediate attendants, not only menials and petty

(*a*) See F. W. Maitland, Introduction to Select Pleas in Manorial Courts. Seld. Soc. 1889; G. H. Blakesley, in L. Q. R. v. 113; and the present writer in Harv. Law Rev. xii. 230.

(*b*) This is most conveniently seen in Mr. Bigelow's "Placita Anglo-Normannica."

officials, but the whole body conveniently denoted by modern authors as the *comitatus*. Many of the king's companions were persons of high rank. Perhaps the king's dealings with his own household were more executive than judicial; and I do not know that any definite share in the establishment of organized royal justice can be attributed to this element. We can only say that it counts among the particular functions which go to swell the general volume of royal authority. At any rate the discipline of the king's retinue, enforced by the king's special peace, helped to make the sight and thought of the king as a dispenser of justice familiar. Obviously the same process was taking place on a smaller scale in the courts of private lords. We might have been spared much display of learning and some insoluble questions if modern antiquaries had remembered that men, and especially great men, in the Middle Ages were capable of doing what suited them first and leaving their counsellors to find reasons for it afterwards.

Simultaneously with the definite establishment of the superior courts, or nearly so, the king's domestic jurisdiction itself became specialized in the Court of the Marshalsea. This and its much later offspring the Palace Court—an offspring which passed for legitimate by courtesy rather than by common right—have a curious little modern history which it will be more convenient to mention at the end of this lecture.

It is not part of my design to recapitulate particulars of our judicial history which are well known and easily verified. Blackstone, who is generally to be trusted after the middle of the thirteenth century, would suffice for the main outlines; but I am the more dispensed from any vain repetition because the "diversity of courts," as our old books say, and the growth and vicissitudes of their several jurisdictions, are now concisely and excellently set forth in a volume published not long ago by a younger colleague, Mr. W. S. Holdsworth of Oxford. For the present purpose we need only to bear in mind the broad fact that in the course of the thirteenth century we find the king's judicial court separated from the king's general council for affairs of state, and further divided into three branches of King's Bench, Common Pleas or Common Bench (*a*), and Exchequer. If we are to fix a point where the royal jurisdiction becomes ordinary and of common right, it would seem to be given by the issue of writs in set forms to any one of the king's subjects who will pay the proper fee. The suitor who "purchases" a writ, as the official phrase ran, must of course choose at his peril that writ which will avail him in his particular case. It is no business of the court or its officers to see that he gets the right one. That is part of the fundamental methods of the common law; the party can have the law's help only by helping himself first. On these terms, and not otherwise, it is open to all. But if we must have a date to remember, we still cannot find a better than that of Magna Carta, for the text of the charter shows clearly that the king's justice is no longer a matter of favour, and that not even any verbal fiction of its being so will be admitted.

The courts were there, but more was to come. It was not enough, in the almost roadless England of Henry III.'s

(*a*) The "certain place" of Magna Carta did not imply a permanent fixing at one place, but only that the Common Pleas were not to follow the then constant journeyings of the king. The final settlement at Westminster came later by convenience and usage. See Holdsworth, Hist. Eng. Law, i. 75.

and Edward I.'s reigns, that men should be free to come to the king's own personal court which followed him, or to the king's judges who did not follow him but sat in a certain place. Royal justice, if it was to prevail thoroughly, had to go forth and conquer the ancient and less convenient jurisdictions on their own ground. Here again an extraordinary and occasional but recognized procedure was available for transformation into a regular and ordinary system of justice, brought, comparatively speaking, to the suitor's own door, but intimately connected with the central authority. The justices in eyre and their successors the justices of assize did more than carry the advantages of the superior jurisdiction (*a*) into every part of England. They saved us from a multiplicity of co-ordinate and independent tribunals which would scarcely have been strong enough to hold their ground at the end of the thirteenth century, and surely would have been too weak to hold it in the middle of the sixteenth, against a wholesale reception of Romanized learning. It was an ancient function of the king, whether regarded as privilege or as public duty, to supervise the administration of justice either by journeys in person (*b*) or by the visits of commissioners. We have an account of Alfred's activity in this kind, unhappily much confused by the pseudo-classical ambition of Asser's style, perhaps also by a Welshman's imperfect acquaintance with

(*a*) It is one of our historical curiosities that the technically superior position of a judge of assize was solemnly determined only after the middle of the nineteenth century, and then, one may say, *in corpore vili*. The judgment delivered on that occasion by the late Mr. Justice Willes (*In re Fernandez* (1861), 10 C. B. N. S. 1) is still a classical authority on the whole subject. That most learned and admirable judge directed me to it himself when I was his marshal on the Western Circuit more than thirty years ago.

(*b*) Maine, Early Law and Custom, 179.

the customs of Wessex. The substantial genuineness of Asser's life of Alfred, except the known interpolations of later work, is, I think, finally established by Mr. W. H. Stevenson's critical edition. After the Conquest we find a steady increase of royal missions for various purposes. The Domesday inquest is memorable among these. It is true that it only touches the fringe of any judicial business. King William's clerks were concerned with his revenue first, and with questions of tenure and title merely as incidental to the determination of the accountable estates and persons. Still we may fairly reckon this as a first step. A century later the itinerant justices, organized experimentally but still organized by Henry II., are distinctly judicial officers, but revenue has not ceased to be their care: "The itinerant judge of the twelfth century has much of the commissioner of taxes" (*a*). It is significant that we find a writ of Henry III., to all appearance defining and improving a practice already known, which commands the county court to meet and assist the justices in eyre (*b*). The functions of the county court on these occasions appear to have been of a strictly subordinate and ministerial kind, and not judicial at all; it was answerable for the proper business being laid before the royal commissioners. So far the commissions of itinerant justices might be wider or narrower; they might cover a comprehensive visitation or be limited to the hearing and determining of a single cause. But the Crown's undertaking in Magna Carta to send out justices regularly to take assizes—the possessory actions introduced by the king's remedial justice—caused one

(*a*) Maitland, P. C. for Gloucester, xxvi.
(*b*) Stubbs, S. C. 358.

variety of itinerant jurisdiction to become fixed and ordinary, though the promise was fulfilled in but a half-hearted fashion before the time of Edward I. The Statute of Westminster added to these judges the miscellaneous civil jurisdiction which we still call *nisi prius*, and finally they acquired, with the aid of various other statutes, and under a number of seemingly unconnected authorities, the power of doing complete justice both civil and criminal, somewhat as the early Roman emperors were, in theory, only citizens on whom the Senate and the People had been pleased to accumulate the functions of several offices (*a*). Once consolidated by usage, their circuits became as much a constant part of the judicial system as the sittings of the courts at Westminster; and the old justices in eyre silently disappeared, their work being superseded or supplanted in all its branches. There was no longer an extraordinary delegation of royal power, but an ordinary legal tribunal; and it was understood that the powers with which the judges, at Westminster or on circuit, had been invested could not be varied by the king's sole authority. The judgment must be the judgment of the court, for "the king hath committed and distributed all his whole power of judicature to several Courts of Justice."

(*a*) Blackst. iii. 60; G. J. Turner, "Circuits and Assizes" in Encycl. Laws of England, vol. 3. To this day the commissions are issued substantially in the old forms, but "since 1884 the names of all the judges of the Supreme Court of Judicature have been placed in the various commissions." Coke's concluding observations in the chapter on Justices of Assize and Nisi Prius in his Fourth Institute are still profitable: "It is commonly called a writ of Nisi Prius, but the words of the writ are Si Prius, &c. And albeit the authority of Justices of Assize . . . . hath by Act of Parliament been exceedingly enlarged both in dignity and magnitude of causes, yet they retain their first and original name, albeit Assizes are in these days" (temp. Jac. I.) "very rarely taken before them."

Much of the king's power had gone out of him by the establishment of the courts at Westminster. But no one supposed in the days of Edward I., or long afterwards, that the king's residuary jurisdiction, to use Maine's convenient term, was exhausted. We need not decide whether Henry II.'s reservation to himself and the wise men of the kingdom of cases too hard for his judges (*a*) was intended to cover original applications, or (as I rather think) only to provide for rehearing of matters referred by the judges. Express reservation of the original jurisdiction, which no one doubted, was made, if it was made, only as an abundant caution. With or without special ordinance, the king and his Council were still there, and might still be called on to do extraordinary justice when the law was insufficient, or in the case, by no means infrequent, of the law having spoken, but execution of its judgment being impracticable by ordinary means. Apparently the doctrine commonly held down to the seventeenth century was that a "pre-eminent and royal jurisdiction" remained for the benefit of the subject, and to refuse the exercise of it to "the injuriously afflicted" would be a denial of justice. It was admitted, however, that when "courts of ordinary resort" had once been set up, it was beyond the king's power to alter their jurisdiction, or administer any kind of justice actually contradictory to the rules followed by them. The greatest and most successful exercise of the king's residuary authority in this behalf was the formation of the Court of Chancery, described by William Lambard, an Elizabethan legal antiquary of considerable repute though not a writer of authority, in these terms: "The king did commit to his Chancellor

(*a*) Stubbs, Const. Hist. I. c. xviii. § 163.

(together with the charge of the great seal) his own regal, absolute, and extraordinary pre-eminence of jurisdiction in civil causes, as well for amendment as for supply of the Common Law" (*a*). There was, of course, no such delegation of authority by any single act of institution. It would be rash to say that there was much deliberate policy about the gradual separation of judicial relief in matters of grace from the general administrative work of the king's Council. Undoubtedly, "the Chancellor's jurisdiction is an offshoot from that of the Council," that is, the king exercising his so-called pre-eminent jurisdiction with the advice of his Council, a jurisdiction of which the scope was for a long time very loosely defined. It does not appear that the Chancellor had any individual judicial functions, otherwise than as one of the Council, much before the middle of the fourteenth century, though there may have been a state of transition during which the business was done by the Chancellor but a few other members of the Council were present for form's sake. The Chancellor certainly acquired power to sit alone, or had it confirmed, in 1349; but this did not forthwith exclude the older practice. Cases of what we should now call equitable jurisdiction continued to be taken to the Council till the latter part of the fifteenth century; as, on the other hand, many cases were brought before the Chancellor by bill of complaint which, according to modern practice, would have been dismissed for "want of equity," the plaintiff having, on his own showing, a cause of action at common law, and the only reason for seeking extraordinary relief being the

(*a*) In his "Archeion" (*sic*) of which the dedication to Sir R. Cecil is dated Oct. 1591.

plaintiff's poverty, or the defendant's overbearing influence and "horrible maintenance." A suit for failure to deliver goods, supported merely by a suggestion that the plaintiff is "but a poor man and fearful of sufficient remedy," is perhaps the strongest case recorded (*a*). Indeed we scarcely hear of Equity by name in the early history of the Court. In the twelfth century the writer whom we call Glanvill could speak of the king as wielding the rod of equity to dispense justice to the lowly and meek, but this is a mere vague flourish. In the fourteenth and fifteenth centuries Conscience, and sometimes Reason, were more commonly invoked; the use of the word Reason suggests a connection, which this is not the place to follow, with the scholastic and cosmopolitan doctrine of the Law of Nature, and, strange as it may seem to lawyers who know the developed Chancery procedure, or laymen who have read of its delays in fiction pretty well justified by fact, the court was regarded as the refuge of the poor and afflicted. To be "Protector of the Poor" has ever been a royal attribute; the quasi-paternal power over lunatics and infants, which still exists in a modified form and is administered through the regular machinery of the court, is akin to it. In India this attribute has sunk to an empty honorific title addressed indiscriminately to all superiors; any European gentleman, even an unofficial traveller, may be saluted as *Gharīb-parwar* a dozen times in a day. In medieval England it was still real enough to assist in founding a jurisdiction. The court was also "the altar and sanctuary for such as against the might of rich men, and the countenance of great men, cannot

(*a*) Cal. Proc. Ch. i. xx. Cf. Select Cases in Chancery, Seld. Soc. 1896, pl. 23, 31.

maintain the goodness of their cause" (*a*). So long as these were the supposed reasons for his judicial existence, the Chancellor was naturally prone to magnify his office by surrounding it with a sort of moral halo, while he avoided anything like a legal definition of what he could or would do; and traces of this tendency may be found in the language of writers on equity, and of the court itself, long after the system had become as technical as that of the common law courts. Obviously, too, the residual jurisdiction of the Crown, of which the Chancery was a branch, would be the more imposing if it remained undefined. But this consideration cut both ways. Defeated suitors felt, not that they had played their game according to rule and lost, but that they had been sacrificed to an inscrutable decree of the king's conscience (represented by the Chancellor, whose conscience might be no better than another man's) setting itself above the law. The king's justice, even as the moderator of legal rigour and champion of good conscience, could not remain extraordinary if it was to be stable. Not only suitors but rival practitioners were eager to trip it up; the common lawyers complained that its decrees were dependent on "the conscience and discretion of the hearers thereof," and that they decided either according to the Civil Law, which had no authority in this realm, or to their own conscience. The only way left was for equity to become a special kind of law and not a discretion capable of subverting law.

In fact, it was settled beyond doubt in 1614 that, as the king had finally delegated his common law jurisdiction to

(*a*) Holdsworth, 206, citing a tract ascribed (it seems without warrant) to Lord Ellesmere, but at any rate of his time.

the courts at Westminster, and for certain limited purposes to the Chancellor, so he had finally delegated his jurisdiction to do Equity to the Court of Chancery. "The King cannot grant a commission to determine any matter of equity, but it ought to be determined in the Court of Chancery, which hath had jurisdiction in such case time out of mind." So, we are told, Lord Ellesmere resolved, assisted by Coke, then lately translated from the Common Pleas to the King's Bench, two puisne justices and the Master of the Rolls; and it had already been held in Elizabeth's time that the queen could not set up a new court of equity by letters patent (*a*). Meanwhile a fierce and vexatious conflict had been raging for many years between the Chancellor, endeavouring to do complete justice, and the judges of the common law courts, who regarded him as an arbitrary intruder putting his "sickle in another man's crop," as Bracton would have said. The story has been lately retold by an accomplished American lawyer, though not for a strictly professional purpose. Judge Phelps of Baltimore has made a most ingenious use of it to clear up Falstaff's remark—at first sight pointless to the modern reader—about "no equity stirring" (*b*). What concerns us now is the ground taken by the law officers of James I., in the spring of 1616, when they were required to advise whether the Statute of Præmunire restrained the Court of Chancery from giving equitable relief against a judgment "lawful and good by the rigour and strict rules of the

(*a*) Coke, 4 Inst. 87, 213; the report in 12 Rep. 114 (a book of inferior authority, as is well known) may be accepted with this corroboration, and I use its words.

(*b*) Falstaff and Equity, by Charles E. Phelps, Boston and New York: 1901. See L. Q. R. xvii. 322.

common law." In an opinion presumably drafted by Bacon, then Attorney-General, they declared, amongst other points, that "the Chancery is a court of ordinary justice for matter of equity, and the statute meant only to restrain extraordinary commissions, and such like proceedings" (*a*). The king's decree made upon this opinion —a personal act of prerogative—upheld the jurisdiction of the Chancellor. There were attempts to dispute it afterwards, but they were feeble and quite ineffectual (*b*).

Undoubtedly the king would not have commanded Lord Ellesmere to send a case to the law officers unless both Lord Ellesmere and himself had known what the opinion would be; we may safely assume, too, that the opinion was framed in a manner intended to be pleasing to James I., and perhaps to some extent on lines of his own suggestion. Our result, then, is that both king and Chancellor found the surest way of maintaining the equitable jurisdiction was to lay down that the Chancery was a regular and ordinary court of justice. Bacon, probably, was not sorry to turn against Coke the declaration in which he had concurred with Lord Ellesmere only two years before. However that may be, the fixity and regularity of the jurisdiction were established, and within about a generation received conclusive professional recognition in the publication of reported decisions, though it must be confessed that the early Chancery reports are of no great merit. After this it was only a matter of time for Bacon's successors to put the house of Equity in order, and make her, as Wallace says, "the intelligent companion

(*a*) Bacon, Letters and Life, ed. Spedding, V. 389, 393.
(*b*) Holdsworth, 250.

instead of the arbitrary mistress of the common law." Modern equity was certainly in its infancy in Blackstone's time; still Blackstone could say truly that "the system of our courts of equity is a laboured connected system, governed by established rules, and bound down by precedents from which they do not depart" (*a*). The genius of our law deliberately prefers the risk of some hardship in particular cases to the unlimited dangers of arbitrary discretion; and in this general principle, as well in various and more specific matters, equity follows the law. So completely has it forgotten its old claim to administer natural justice that a judge of the Chancery Division in England can now say, "This Court is not a Court of Conscience" (*b*).

Thus did the Chancellor's equitable jurisdiction become, and declare itself to be, regular and ordinary, as a condition of being acquiesced in by the other courts and accepted by the Commonwealth. But this was not all. The Chancery had to make large concessions to the common law in its procedure. That procedure was founded on the summary process of the canon law (not directly on the civil law), and was originally inquisitorial. Perhaps the most striking deviation of a suit in equity from a typical action at common law is the power of the court to examine the parties on oath, a power absolutely unlike anything at the disposal of the King's Bench or the Common Pleas. This, like all the rest of the proceedings from first to last, was, in theory, under the direction and control of the court, which might and sometimes did take evidence on its own

(*a*) Comm. iii. 432, cf. Williams, R. P. 19th ed. 163.
(*b*) [1903] 2 Ch. 195.

account "to inform the conscience of the judge" (*a*). But we find that these functions of the court were already handed over to the parties when equity procedure became settled, and the procedure, though differing much in form from that of the common law courts, was in substance no less contentious. The Chancellors had resisted all attempts to introduce the rules of common law pleading, but no one who has made acquaintance with equity pleadings even in their latest reformed shape can charge them with having failed to stiffen themselves with sufficient technical rules of their own. What concerns us here, however, is that the judge's authority to inform himself became the litigant's right to obtain discovery from his adversary. Much of the work of modern courts of equity, as all lawyers know, is not litigious at all, but administrative, though it may involve decision between conflicting claims, and thus lead to the settlement of disputed points of law. But even this was not distinguished in form from the ordinary contentious jurisdiction. It may be doubted whether the operations of the court in administering estates did not suffer in both speed and efficiency from this refusal or failure to discriminate between really different functions. The facts, at any rate, show the strength of the Germanic tradition which insists on regarding the court as an umpire between parties.

Meanwhile the "pre-eminent" or supra-legal jurisdiction of the king in Council survived for a considerable time. It

(*a*) Spence i. 380, calling this "a strange practice," which it is from the English but not from the Continental point of view. The practice of taking evidence in writing, though widespread in modern Romanist systems, is no necessary part of the civilian or canonical scheme: Langdell, Equity Pleading, sec. 8.

took another specialized form in the Court of Requests, originally a poor man's court of equity. This court passed through a sharp conflict with the judges of the common law, to whom it was unable to oppose the justification of ancient origin. They could not deny that it was useful, and Coke himself suggested statutory regulation. After a short time of revived activity in the reign of Charles I. the court perished in the general ruin of the Privy Council's extraordinary jurisdictions, and no attempt was made to set it up again at the Restoration. It seems to have been a pure misadventure that it failed to develop into a regular court of equity, whose relations to the Court of Chancery might have been adjusted later without much trouble, and with no small benefit for suitors. A modern Master of the Requests would have been in name a dignified and fitting companion to the Master of the Rolls, and in fact quite as useful as the Vice-Chancellor who had to be invented much later. For our purpose the moral is that irregular courts, in the lands of the common law, are not tolerated in the long run even when they are innocent. The vicissitudes and downfall of the Star Chamber and other branches of the jurisdiction exercised by the king in Council will be better considered under the head of the relations of the common law to criminal justice and executive power.

One court might claim, down to modern times, to represent the king's original personal justice more directly than the superior courts of common law and even the Chancellor. This was the Marshalsea, the special court of the king's household wielding archaic and limited jurisdiction over its members; it does not seem to have had anything to do with the King's Council. Its more obvious defects of jurisdiction were supplemented by a new court, entitled "The Court of the Lord the King, at the Palace of the King at Westminster," created by several letters patent of James I., Charles I., and finally Charles II. These courts appear to have almost escaped professional criticism, partly because their jurisdiction was merely local, partly because their process followed substantially the course of the common law. At any rate the final charter of Charles II. was not disputed; and the Marshalsea, moreover, rested on the firm ground of prescription. We learn, however, from the only writer on the practice of these courts, that the Palace Court had quite superseded it by the beginning of the 19th century at latest; the two courts purported to be opened together, but the Marshalsea did no business. He that would know the true causes of the fall of the Palace Court may find them set down as well in a very useful modern book of reference (*a*) as by a layman whose name was Thackeray in the Ballads of Policeman X., under the heading of "Jacob Homnium's Hoss: a Pallice Court chaunt." Like most petty local courts the Palace Court became a hotbed of abuses; and, although error would lie to the King's Bench, the remedy of a new trial was not available to correct a perverse verdict. Such verdicts were not uncommon, for the juries were apparently drawn from the small tradesman class, and invariably found for a tradesman plaintiff whatever the evidence and the law might be. The court was abolished in 1849, and therewith, it would seem, the last relic of the only royal jurisdiction which had never passed through the hands of the Council.

Long before the accession of James I. the king's justice

(*a*) Enc. Laws of Eng. *s. v.* Palace Court.

had, as we have seen, become regular and had been delegated to his judges. If James I. had been as prudent as his English ancestors, he would have tacitly accepted the fact that the delegation was irrevocable. But James I. had theories of royal power in general and his own royal wisdom in particular; and he willingly gave ear when, being jealous of the common law courts and their prohibitions, Archbishop Bancroft encouraged him to claim the right of taking an active part in judicial proceedings (*a*). The view suggested was "that the judges are but the delegates of the King, and that the King may take what causes he shall please to determine from the determination of the judges, and may determine them himself." This drew from the judges, speaking by Coke, a solemn declaration "that the King in his own person cannot adjudge any case," but all causes, whether criminal or civil, "ought to be determined and adjudged in some court of justice, according to the law and custom of England." The king may sit in the King's Bench if he likes, but the court gives the judgment. Perhaps it is not commonly known that an empty seat is to this day reserved for the king at the Council Board at

(*a*) The introductory statement in Coke's Reports is neither full nor clear, and the substance of the report is by no means free from doubt. It is not consistent in detail with other contemporary accounts, and there is reason to think that Coke ascribed to himself more firmness and dignity than he showed in fact, and that either he or the editor of his imperfectly digested materials mixed up incidents which took place at different times. It is far from certain that a set argument such as is suggested by the references to authorities was ever addressed to the king at all. See "James I. and Sir Edward Coke," by Roland G. Usher, Eng. Hist. Rev. xviii. 664. The important thing for us, however, is the opinion of Coke and his colleagues, and there can be no doubt that this is correctly given. For the connected story of these transactions, see Gardiner, Hist. Eng. ii. 38.

Whitehall; if it were his pleasure to occupy it during a sitting of the Judicial Committee, he would be as merely a spectator—though a specially honoured one—as any stranger present. Thus we owe the positive definition of what might well have been left as a "constitutional understanding" partly to James I. and partly to a not very wise archbishop; "it was greatly marvelled that the Archbishop durst inform the King that such absolute power and authority, as is aforesaid, belonged to the King by the word of God" (*a*). Still less could the king act in person in the executive part of justice, as the judges triumphantly showed James I. in the Year Book of Henry VII. The reason is highly characteristic of the common law. "Hussey, Chief Justice, said that Sir John Markham (Chief Justice of the King's Bench) said to King Edward IV. that he could not arrest a man on suspicion of treason or felony as any of his subjects could, because if he did wrong the party could not have an action" (*b*). Here it is assumed without remark that any person, official or not, acting under the king's orders would be amenable to the ordinary process of law if his action were not justified. If the king's officer could not be liable to an action, but only to some form of discipline outside the ordinary jurisdiction, or indeed if such a position could be thought arguable, Markham's saying would obviously have no point at all. Even the servants of the king and the law must take the risk of being wrong; and since the king may not risk anything, he also must not play the game. A rather nice question might arise if a felony were actually committed in the king's presence and there were no one else

(*a*) 12 Co. Rep. 63—65.

(*b*) 1 H. VII. 4, pl. 5. Hussey is the modern form of this Chief Justice's family name; it appears that in his time it was written Huse.

to arrest the felon; but this is not known ever to have occurred. As for the good archbishop's conception of judicial authority, it was essentially civilian. It would have made the king the real judge and the judges his clerks. The relation which Bancroft fondly imagined to exist between James I. and Coke is that which really does exist in equity practice between the judge and the Master or Chief Clerk (*a*), where there is, properly, not an appeal from the Master's certificate, but a rehearing before the judge in person.

As judicature belongs exclusively to the judges, so does the interpretation of the law. This has never been disputed. We cannot positively say that Bracton held our modern doctrine as to the authority of judicial decisions; but we can safely say with Mr. Maitland, since Mr. Maitland has given us Bracton's note-book, that his law is case law. Early in the fourteenth century it was recognized in court that the decisions of the court would be used as authority; a century and a half later the judges were discussing, almost as we might now, what special circumstances would justify them in departing from a previous decision in point. As to the construction of Acts of Parliament, the judges easily took up a commanding position. Who should know best what a statute meant, if not the judges who had themselves been consulted in framing it? "We know it better than you, for it was our work," said Hengham, C. J., to counsel discussing the Statute of Westminster (*b*). Modern judges are more apt to protest that modern statutes have been made by incompetent workmen,

(*a*) This official title was in use for many years in England, but is now abolished.

(*b*) References in Pollock, First Book of Jurisprudence, 301, 302, 331.

or, as oftener happens, marred by incompetent amenders before they finally passed. So complete is the detachment of the judicial from the legislative function that noble and learned members of the House of Lords have severely censured, in the exercise of the former, the language of an Act for which they were themselves answerable in the latter capacity. This, it will be observed, is, in the mother country at any rate, purely the effect of professional custom. It has nothing to do with any enactment or modern constitutional rule; it is the completed outcome of our very ancient Germanic principle that the court finds its own law.

A great and novel development of this principle has taken place in the jurisprudence of the United States. It is mainly due to the commanding genius of John Marshall. The best and shortest expression of it I have found is in the words of the late Mr. Phelps, a true scholar, a brilliant lawyer and a profound statesman (*a*). "It is upon the intrusting to the judicial department of the whole subject of the constitutional law, for all purposes, that our government rests," and, "that point once established by the court, the simple, the ancient, the salutary, the perfectly intelligible and just principles of the common law became sufficient for all the purposes of constitutional construction." The venerable traditions and the living vigour of our law are combined in the highest degree by the judicial authority of the Supreme Court interpreting the Constitution of the United States as the supreme law of the land.

(*a*) Orations and Essays of Edward John Phelps, New York and London, 1901, pp. 41, 42.

III. The Sword of Justice.

In the repression of crime and the active execution of the law we find a sequence from earlier to later times closely parallel to that which we have already noticed in civil jurisdiction. The King's power is at first held in reserve to be exercised only on occasions of special urgency. But, as government is consolidated, resort to the King's justice is more and more common, until it becomes the rule, and the cumbrous methods of the old popular courts are superseded. Remedies which were extraordinary become ordinary; the jurisdiction is accepted as regular, and recognized, by statutory amendment, and otherwise, in the proceedings of Parliament. But in thus becoming an everyday affair the royal jurisdiction has lost something of its ancient moral authority. Great men despise the process and executive officers even of the King's justice; poor men complain that the local influence of their powerful adversaries makes it impossible for them to get anything done. Sheriffs are cajoled or bribed; juries are often packed, sometimes bribed and sometimes intimidated. New kinds of wrongdoing, public and private, which cannot be dealt with under any of the fixed forms of the Common Law, disturb the peace of the kingdom and vex honest men. Fresh exercise of the King's residuary power is the obvious remedy. The King and the Council cannot recall or refashion the judicial functions already created; but they can supplement the shortcomings of the regular process of law; they would not be performing their duty to the kingdom if they did not. Enormous offences call for a greater axe. Down to the reign of Charles I. this was accepted doctrine. It is allowed by all recent writers on the subject that the extraordinary criminal jurisdiction of the King's Council sitting in the Star Chamber (such was the proper style (*a*)), criminal equity, as it has been called, was analogous to the equitable jurisdiction of the Chancellor in civil matters, as the best contemporary authorities said it was.

But extra-judicial causes, reinforced by barely plausible legal reasons only as an afterthought, led to complete divergence in the results. The "prætorian" civil jurisdiction flourished and became in due time a perfectly regular part of our judicature; the "censorial" power of the Council, while it was still imperfectly specialized, was abused for the ends of political and religious tyranny, and provoked a reaction which involved it in the general fall of Charles I.'s system of absolute government.

In Henry VIII.'s time, as Sir Thomas Smith, writing under Elizabeth, tells us, it was "marvellous necessary" to augment the authority of the Star Chamber "to repress

(*a*) The opinion that the Star Chamber was a new and illegal court seems to have rested partly on forgetfulness of this material fact and partly on a misunderstanding of the Act of Henry VII. which gave a special jurisdiction to a statutory Commission, including persons who might not be members of the Council. See Coke, 4 Inst. 62; Stephen, Hist. Cr. L. c. vi.; Holdsworth i. 271; Carter, Hist. of English Legal Institutions, c. xiv.; Leadam, Introduction to Select Cases in Star Chamber, Seld. Soc. 1903. It is doubtful whether this statutory court ever acted; see Leadam, *op. cit.* xxxvi., lxv., lxxi. Apparently it might have sat anywhere in England.

the insolency of the noblemen and gentlemen of the north parts of England, who being far from the King and the seat of justice made almost as it were an ordinary war among themselves, and made their force their law, banding themselves with their tenants and servants to do or revenge injury one against another as they listed." Coke, a stern enough censor of encroaching jurisdictions, called the Star Chamber "the most honourable court (our Parliament excepted) that is in the Christian world," and added: "This court, the right institution and ancient orders thereof being observed, doth keep all England quiet." It is remarkable that Coke has nothing to say about the Star Chamber's very wide departure from the course of the Common Law. He states without any comment that "the proceeding in this court is by bill or information, by examination of the defendant upon interrogatories, and by examination of witnesses." Perhaps he thought that sufficient respect was paid to the Common Law, and good enough security taken for substantial justice being observed, by the inclusion of the two chief justices among the ordinary members of the court. At any rate Coke's testimony removes any suspicion of partiality that might otherwise attach to Bacon's. What Bacon says is worth citing in full, both as a good specimen of his prose and as an illustration of the received doctrine of "residual jurisdiction." He says in his History of King Henry VII. (*a*) :—

"* * * There were that Parliament [A. D. 1487] divers excellent laws ordained. * * *

"First, the authority of the Star Chamber, which before subsisted by the ancient common laws of the realm, was

(*a*) Works, ed. Spedding, vi. 85.

confirmed in certain cases by Act of Parliament. This court is one of the sagest and noblest institutions of this kingdom. For in the distribution of courts of ordinary justice (besides the High Court of Parliament), in which distribution the King's Bench holdeth the pleas of the Crown; the Common-place, pleas civil; the Exchequer, pleas concerning the King's revenues; and the Chancery, the Pretorian power for mitigating the rigour of law, in case of extremity, by the conscience of a good man; there was nevertheless always reserved a high and pre-eminent power to the King's counsel in causes that might in example or consequence concern the state of the commonwealth; which, if they were criminal, the counsel used to sit in the chamber called the Star Chamber; if civil, in the White-chamber or White-hall. And as the Chancery had the Pretorian power for equity, so the Star Chamber had the Censorian power for offences under the degree of capital. This court of Star Chamber is compounded of good elements; for it consisteth of four kinds of persons: counsellors, peers, prelates and chief justices; it discerneth also principally of four kinds of causes: forces, frauds, crimes various of stellionate (*a*), and the inchoations or middle acts towards crimes capital or heinous not actually committed or perpetrated. But that which was principally aimed at by this act was force (*suppressio turbarum illicitarum*, Latin version) and the two chief supports of force, combination of multitudes, and maintenance or headship of great persons."

Thus the Council in the Star Chamber, like the Chancellor in his court, dealt partly with offences for which

(*a*) *Stellionatus* is in Roman law criminal fraud not amounting to any other definite offence: Dig. XLVII. 20, Cod. IX. 34.

there was an adequate remedy in fact in the ordinary course of law, partly with such as were not otherwise punishable at all, or not clearly so. Riot and unlawful assemblies, intimidation, forgery, miscellaneous frauds and perjury were the staple matters of its jurisdiction. There is no reason to doubt that for many years the activity of the Star Chamber was useful and even popular. It is at least doubtful whether its sentences were commonly thought too severe until it began to make itself an instrument of political persecution. In many cases the offence had been denounced, and the punishment prescribed, by Act of Parliament. It does not appear that anyone protested against the absence of a jury. Defendants did object to being interrogated on oath by the court. On this point it may perhaps be doubted whether systematic and deliberate interrogation were less fair to a man on his trial than the running fire of cross-examination by the judges, restrained by no rules of evidence, which the prisoner had to stand in all ordinary criminal cases of any importance down to the Restoration. There was, however, then and long afterwards, a much sharper distinction in common opinion between sworn and unsworn assertions or answers than any honest man would now admit. An unknown man's oath seems to have weighed a good deal more with our ancestors than it does with us, and his word a good deal less. "One man's oath is as good as another's," was the current opinion till the second quarter of the eighteenth century. We may even read how the reason that "the law intends the oath of every man to be true" was seriously assigned for perjury being a merely statutory offence (*a*). An interesting

(*a*) Prof. Wigmore in Harv. Law Rev. xv. 89 *sqq.*; Stephen, Hist. Cr. L. iii. 245.

but insoluble question is what would have been the effect on our ideas and practice in the matter of criminal justice if the Star Chamber had persisted. Certainly the modern sentiment which says to the twelve men in a box "Ye are gods," could not have grown up such as we have it now. We may guess, on the other hand, that the obnoxious inquisitorial process would have come into subjection to the rules of evidence, and have been modified into something no worse than making the accused a compellable as well as a competent witness on his own behalf. The competition of the Star Chamber might even have led to improvements in the practice of the ordinary courts for which, as it fell out, we had to wait till the nineteenth century. But all this is mere speculation. Under Charles I. there was a well-known series of really tyrannical prosecutions for so-called libels which would now be left to the mercies of serious or comic reviewers. The excessive sentences on Prynne and others brought the Star Chamber into hopeless disrepute. Yet the Act of 1640 which abolished the court did not deny the jurisdiction. The preamble does indeed suggest that it was derived merely from the Act of Henry VII., a view which no one now thinks defensible; it goes on to charge the court with having invented new offences, which was true to some extent, but justifiable according to the received opinion of the King's powers and duties; with having inflicted "heavier punishments than by any law is warranted," which seems doubtful, considering the number and ferocity of sixteenth-century penal statutes; and with having abused its process "to introduce an arbitrary power and government," which was certainly true. Not only "the court commonly called the Star Chamber" but other similar jurisdictions were severally and collectively abolished, and any attempt to erect any such "court council or judicature" forbidden for time to come. The Council of the North, the Council of Wales and the Marches, and minor jurisdictions of the same kind in the Duchy of Lancaster and county palatine of Chester—all being in the nature of criminal equity modelled on the Star Chamber practice, and having more or less statutory confirmation to show—were expressly included. In terms the abolition did not extend to the Court of Requests, which administered only civil justice; nevertheless its position became untenable, and, as we have seen, it disappeared (*a*). Thus did the Star Chamber and its satellites fall upon the common law, and they were broken. After the Restoration the Court of King's Bench assumed, without objection from anyone, those parts of the Star Chamber jurisdiction which were of obvious general utility, besides the more doubtful attribute of a general censorial power over publications. This quasi-judicial control of the press appears to be the principal historical origin of our modern law of copyright. It is beyond our present scope to say anything of the manner in which the subject became a battle-ground for speculative arguments derived from the eighteenth-century version of the Law of Nature, and the problem was quieted though not solved by a statutory compromise.

It is significant for our purpose that the growth of the Star Chamber and kindred jurisdictions coincides with the period in which the business and reputation of the common law courts were at their lowest point, and in which the Year Books came to an obscure end. There were men in high

(*a*) Sir James Stephen points out that the other courts named in the Act were not abolished, but only their jurisdiction so far as it was like that of the Star Chamber. The effect was abolition.

places who would have well liked to see Henry VIII. attempt a reception of Roman law in England; if there was not a formed plot against the common law, there were all the materials for it. So my learned friend Mr. Maitland has told us with his peculiar felicity (*a*). He thinks the danger was really considerable; he is disposed to ascribe its brief duration and the vigorous reaction that followed to the existence of a school of national law in the Inns of Court. We cannot actually prove a deliberate policy of depressing the ordinary courts with a view to supplant their more important functions by extraordinary jurisdictions and at last reduce them to insignificance; but it is a case of grave suspicion. At all events the impression made on a student of political history coming to the subject with a fresh mind is that the policy of the King's Council under the Tudors was directed to impressing and did impress even the ordinary course of criminal justice with an inquisitorial character (*b*).

If we believe, however, that the course of the events which determine national issues is above the individual will and design of any actor in them, and that the reasons assigned by the best observers at the time, even if really operative, are seldom the whole or the most efficient, we shall regard it as a secondary question whether there was at any time a settled plan for subordinating the maintenance of public order in the King's name and by a regular system of legal justice to an extraordinary royal power which would have professed to do justice but which claimed to be superior to the law. The conflict was in fact as acute and as decisive

(*a*) English Law and the Renaissance, Cambridge, 1901.
(*b*) John Pollock, The Popish Plot, 289.

as if it had been deliberately prepared on both sides. Bacon had talked of lions under the throne. Before another generation had passed, all men might see that the Common Law was on the throne and the King's prerogative was under it. Beware how you touch points of prerogative, said James I., with Bacon's advice and approval. Prerogative is nothing but the law specially concerning the King, said Selden, and so we have all said after him.

The undefined powers of the Crown in matters of executive policy have had a different history. They have not been suppressed; they have been very little if at all impaired. They have been taken alive by a Ministry existing at the will of the House of Commons, and have enabled us to combine a democratic legislature with an executive which, when it chooses to act boldly, can be as swift and strong as any in the world. We can afford to trust our ministers with the ancient rights of the Crown, including the right to make war and peace and conclude treaties, because they can be called to account at any moment. At the time when the constitutional position of the judicature and the autonomy of the superior courts were settled, the political doctrine of ministerial responsibility was not yet known. If it had come earlier, the Star Chamber jurisdiction might have been transformed instead of being abolished; the House of Commons would, in one form or another, have interfered more actively and frequently in judicial affairs; and the appellate jurisdiction of Parliament, which as late as the Restoration was neither defined nor clearly recognized, might have been shared in some way between the two Houses instead of being confined to the House of Lords. It might be an amusing speculation whether this kind of development would have given us better or worse law than we have. I rather think it would have tended to make the courts too sensitive to political influence and the current theories of the day. Social, economical and political doctrines do leave their mark, as it is, on our unwritten law; but the movement is gradual. In about three centuries we have practically reversed our working rule about agreements in restraint of trade, and this without a breach of continuity at any assignable point and without any aid from legislation. The mill has ground slowly but small. Would the result have been as convincing if it had been less deliberate or less detached from politics?

But let us leave guesswork. The capital fact for us is that the machinery of the King's Peace, from the Court of King's Bench to the rustic justice of petty sessions, was consolidated, between the twelfth and the sixteenth centuries, out of powers in their origin special and extraordinary; and that, having become ordinary, it was strong enough to hold its own against arbitrary additions even when they came with no small colour of public utility. How had the King's justice won the whole field and become popular in its victory? The conquest was almost dramatic in thoroughness and speed. In the first half of the twelfth century one might still talk of the blood-feud as the normal way of pursuing crime, and the nascent pleas of the Crown, the matters reserved to the jurisdiction of the King, or those lords to whom he granted royal franchises, as exceptional. By the end of that century the proceedings in serious criminal cases were already in the King's hand, or, if not initiated in his name, largely under his control (*a*). The methods of proof were still archaic, but improvement was beginning.

(*a*) See 13 Harv. Law Rev. 77 *sqq.*

The ancient popular justice had broken down. The strong point of its methods was a very summary process when the criminal was caught red-handed. How that process became obsolete is not quite clear. A peculiar jurisdiction to punish theft in this manner, the mode of execution being decapitation by a kind of guillotine, existed under a local franchise at Halifax in Yorkshire as late as the eighteenth century, though the last instance of its exercise appears to have been in 1650 (*a*). But, failing this first chance, there were no satisfactory means in the popular procedure of convicting the guilty or clearing accused innocent persons, and no regular means at all of detecting criminals or bringing suspected persons to trial. The law had only the precarious and clumsy instruments of ordeal and outlawry. The formal condemnation of ordeal by the Church brought matters to a crisis. Perhaps the Lateran Council only set an official stamp on a practically foregone conclusion. There is clear enough proof that in England the ordeal was already discredited before the end of the twelfth century. Clerkly writers were quite prepared to hint their belief in a condemned man's innocence if a miracle had been wrought for him afterwards, as we find in a very celebrated case in the acts of St. Thomas of Canterbury. Moreover, the Church had in truth (and this should be remembered to her credit)

(*a*) Halifax and its Gibbet-law placed in a true light. Lond. 1708, republished at Halifax in 1761. The first edition seems not to have been known to Sir James Stephen, whose account, Hist. Cr. L. i. 265, is sufficient for most purposes. The felon had to be taken "hand-habend, back-berand, or confessand," conditions which seem to have been rather loosely interpreted. The so-called jurymen were not a sworn inquest, but represented the ancient witness of the suitors, and were themselves the judges "to hear, examine and determine."

never liked the ordeal in any form. If the water and the iron had their garnish of clerkly pomp and ritual, this was allowed for the hardness of men's hearts, and moreover gave opportunities of controlling the result which were almost certainly used, and probably used, on the whole, on the side of substantial justice. Whether the ordeal was driven out by the Lateran Council or merely expedited on the way it was already going, it disappeared, and a new mode of final trial had to be found.

One instrument of justice was still recent, favoured as an enlightened invention, and capable of fresh adaptations. The contact of royal authority with popular courts had already turned the vague accusation of offenders by common report into a presentment by definite persons chosen to represent the best knowledge of the neighbourhood. Already the verdict of a new or reinforced jury had been taken as equivalent to the conclusive proof against a criminal afforded by manifest facts. The red-handed manslayer or "hand-having" thief taken on fresh pursuit and with good witness had no defence open to him. "He cannot gainsay it, so let him be hanged." So the judgment of the law still ran in the thirteenth century. It seemed reasonable to some of the King's judges that deliberate confirmation of the accusing inquest by a fresh inquest of the country should be deemed as strong as ocular proof. Henry of Bratton was prepared to make trial by the country the universal and compulsory process. Most unfortunately for the credit of the law this direct and simple way was not taken. Criminal procedure admitted, in the Anglo-Norman period, of three ways of decision. First, summary condemnation and execution upon the suitors' direct witness of the crime. This went out of use in the course of the thirteenth century. Secondly, ordeal. This, as we said, was formally abolished. Thirdly, battle (in principle a kind of ordeal, as being the judgment of God, but having a quite distinct history), in the case, and in such case only, of an "appeal" by a widow or kinsman. This criminal appeal was really a legalized form of the blood-feud, and preserved traces of private revenge long after the enforcement of the sentence had been taken over by public justice. As late as 1409 Justice Tirwhit said, "By the ancient law when one is hanged on an appeal of a man's death, the dead man's wife and all his kin shall drag the felon to execution"; and Chief Justice Gascoigne added "That has been so in our own time" (*a*). But in the case of the appellor dying or making default the suit passed over to the King, as the wrong included a breach of the King's peace, and the King could not do battle. For the rest, trial by battle remained possible in some civil cases, but it appears, from the early thirteenth century onwards, mostly as a cloak for a compromise made at the last moment. We hear of settlements when the champions were in the field, and of the court, by way of getting some sport for their trouble, requiring the champions to exchange a few strokes for form's sake. Archaic as it undoubtedly was (*b*), trial by battle was never anything but an unpopular exotic in England. It lingered as a mere curiosity of the law till the early part of the nineteenth century, when an unexpected revival of the right to demand it in a criminal

(*a*) 11 Henry IV. 12, pl. 24.

(*b*) The horned staff which was the proper weapon of the judicial duel may even point (though this is doubtful) to an origin earlier than the use of metals. Observe that the knightly duel of the later Middle Ages is entirely distinct, and see generally Mr. G. Neilson's excellent monograph, "Trial by Combat."

appeal brought about its formal abolition. The story is very well known, and it would be useless for our present purpose to recall it here. Finally, trial by the country was introduced early in the thirteenth century as an alternative at the prisoner's option. The natural and reasonable course would have been to send him to a jury without option in the cases, becoming the majority, where no other mode of trial was possible. But our criminal law had already hardened into so much formalism that, notwithstanding the better example of Bracton and others, the judges disclaimed jurisdiction to summon a jury to try a prisoner who had not put himself on the country. The nominal option was not to be touched, although there was no real alternative left. Accordingly the prisoner who "stood mute" brought the whole proceeding to a deadlock. Nothing better occurred to the champions of logic and abhorrers of usurped jurisdiction than to treat his conduct as a contempt of the King's authority, very nearly though not quite amounting to a capital offence; and this led, after a short period of unsettled practice, to the "peine forte et dure." The barbarous pedantry of turning the prisoner's right to choose his own mode of trial into an election to save his property or his conscience, as the motive might be, by suffering a cruel and contumelious death, was the worst blot on our criminal system (*a*), and remained so for centuries. Neither the solution of treating the prisoner as guilty by default, nor the more benignant

(*a*) English criminal law in general, as it was in the Middle Ages, may seem cruel to those who do not know anything of Continental methods. To those who do it will appear, as it did to Fortescue, relatively humane. There is a heavy debit to the account of Roman example and learning in this matter.

fiction, which we have now adopted, of treating him as having pleaded not guilty, occurred to anyone. Much bolder fictions were to be used in time by the judges of the several courts to extend their jurisdiction; but perhaps we may say that in the thirteenth century the age of fictions good or bad was not yet. However, the case of a prisoner refusing to plead was not common, though we hear of it down to the eighteenth century; nor has it any traceable connexion with the general evolution of the law.

On the whole the jury triumphed in criminal as well as in civil justice, partial anomalies notwithstanding. But until the sixteenth century the process was gradual and inconspicuous, and some of the most important matters were settled as it were by accident. We can now see that if the verdict of a majority had been accepted, the resistance of juries to the Crown in later times would have been perhaps impossible, certainly much less effective. The rule was not fixed before the fourteenth century, and I do not think it was ever laid down in terms that juries must be unanimous. It is true that the dooms of the ancient popular courts had in some countries, if not in England, to be unanimous; but the jury has nothing to do with the ancient folk-law. What was actually decided was that the verdict of fewer than twelve men would not do, and this appears to rest on a quite different, but not less archaic principle, the inherent sanctity of the number twelve. Then, as not less than twelve men would suffice, so it became the fixed custom not to have more on a petit jury; why I know not, unless that it obviously saved trouble to take the least number that sufficed. To this day the grand jury need not be unanimous, though every presentment must be made by at least twelve men. Accordingly the total number is twenty-three, making twelve a majority. During the formative period nobody that I know of had any inkling of the future political and constitutional importance of jury trial. Fortescue's panegyric on the twelve men in his "De laudibus legum Angliae" is a learned, artificial and, I fear, scarcely honest panegyric addressed, like the whole treatise, to exalting the Common Law above the Civil Law. The ordinary English suitor naturally knew nothing about foreign civilian procedure, and therefore could not appreciate what he had escaped. He might know something of canonical procedure through the spiritual courts. Ecclesiastical officials might be meddling and fussy; but, until late in the fifteenth century, the Courts Christian, under colour of punishing the sin of breach of faith, provided remedies in many cases of ordinary secular business which the King's justices regarded as outside their jurisdiction. There is no reason to think that Fortescue represented public opinion or troubled himself about it, or that the verdicts of juries were then particularly respected or trusted in common esteem. Indeed, the Paston letters and the early Chancery records more than suggest the contrary. At the beginning of the fifteenth century we find a defendant, presumably a powerful man, denounced not only as a maintainer and extortioner, but as a corrupter of juries—"Conducour des enquestes en sa pays" (*a*). With the Renaissance there came a spirit of comparative inquiry and something more like impartial criticism. Sir Thomas Smith commended the jury process, not because it necessarily led to a right judgment on the merits, for

(*a*) Select Cases in Chancery, Selden Soc. pl. 51.

"the twelve men be commonly rude and ignorant," but because it was more expeditious than the interminable written pleading of the civilians. The first virtue of legal justice, in a society still subject to disorders, is not that it decides rightly, but that it decides at all. We have now almost forgotten this.

What really made the fortune of the jury was the excessive zeal of royal officers in the Tudor period. For a time they made Parliament little more than an instrument for registering royal decrees; next they wanted to make jurymen passive registrars of foregone political condemnations, and that was too much. A fixed point is given by the acquittal of Sir Nicholas Throckmorton, under Queen Mary, on the charge of high treason by complicity in Wyatt's rebellion. Against the Crown and against the court the jury found him not guilty, partly persuaded by his extremely able defence, and partly, one may guess, because the citizens of London at large "misliked the coming of the Spaniards into this realm" no less than Sir Nicholas himself. True, the jurors were reprimanded and some of them fined: but, as Sir Thomas Smith, no demagogue, tells us, "those doings were even then of many accounted very violent, tyrannical, and contrary to the liberty and custom of the realm of England." From that time the power of juries, and their function as the voice of public feeling, began to be understood; and they became capable not only of guarding the liberty of the subject, but of contributing priceless elements of common sense and business knowledge to the development of the Common Law in civil jurisdiction. On the whole they reflected common opinion faithfully enough, for better or worse. There was no warrant against a jury being misled by panic or prejudice. It fared ill with prisoners when the jurymen's political or religious aversions went along with the case for the prosecution, as was seen at the time of the Popish Plot. On the other hand an acquittal in a political prosecution, as in the case of the Seven Bishops, was for the seventeenth century the nearest equivalent to a public meeting of protest, or even to a vote of censure in the modern House of Commons. From a professional point of view it is perhaps still more material that the forms of trial by jury permanently secured the publicity of judicial proceedings. Doubtless it was and is possible to hold a trial by jury with closed doors, and in modern practice it has been done for very special cause. It is even said that the court has inherent jurisdiction to hear any kind of case in private when it is clear that justice cannot be done otherwise (*a*). But, in a general way, publicity is essential, and was so regarded in Sir Thomas Smith's day. It might, at that time, be the only means of completing the evidence. "There is nothing put in writing," he says, "but the indictment only. All the rest is done openly in the presence of the judges, the justices [of the peace], the inquest, the prisoner, and so many as will or can come so near as to hear it, and all depositions and witnesses given aloud, that all men may hear from the mouth of the depositors and witnesses what is said" (*b*). And so, by seemingly devious ways, the jury became, like the ancient courts of the county and hundred, an organ of social and not merely official justice, making sure that justice should be done in the light of day; but, unlike them, it was clear of archaic

(*a*) By Sir Francis Jeune, *D.* v. *D.*, [1903] P. 144.

(*b*) Commonwealth of England, Bk. 2, c. 26. The obvious allusion to *Throckmorton's* case is in Bk. 3, c. 1.

formalities and capable of furnishing material for a true legal science.

Even more instructive is the history of the King's peace in its administrative branch. Originally the King's protection is a matter not of common right but of privilege. Every man is entitled to maintain the peace of his own house; this is a very ancient Germanic principle still echoed in the adage "An Englishman's house is his castle" (*a*). We may trace it in the jealous definition, still not without practical importance, of the occasions that will justify breaking doors open in execution of legal process. Now the King's house is the greatest, and therefore has a special and privileged peace, the breach of which is a grave matter indeed. Gradually this domestic peace extends to the precincts of the King's court, and those precincts are somewhat largely described. Moreover, the King's servants and others about his business, which is the business of the kingdom, enjoy a special protection, and so do those to whom the King, for reasons of which he is himself the judge, has made a particular grant of it. The sanction of the King's peace is used for composing blood-feuds; it reinforces the peace of God, that is, of the Church, at holy seasons; it is extended to markets and to the great roads. Being auxiliary to the King's jurisdiction, it grows with the growth of his judicial powers. At last it is discovered that the privileges once distinct and enumerable have covered the whole ground and been merged in a common rule. One must still expressly invoke the King's peace if one will have

(*a*) In the fourteenth century, if not later, the lord's peace was proclaimed at the opening of manorial courts. Is this a survival of the lord's domestic peace or a mere imitation of royal procedure? The special peace of the Bishop of Durham, and the like, in palatine jurisdictions was a delegation of the King's peace included in *jura regalia*.

the benefit of the King's justice against wrong-doers; but its protection and remedies are to be had as of course when claimed in due form. Every lawful man is in the peace of God and of our lord the King. One inconvenience remained till late in the thirteenth century. The King's peace, considered as a personal protection granted by William or Henry, depended on the King's life and perished at his death. Not being fully King until he was crowned, the new King had no peace of his own in the interval, and the country was remitted to the clumsy and enfeebled resources of the sheriff and the popular courts. Evil-doers had their opportunity and made the most of it. "There was tribulation soon in the land," says the English Chronicle on the death of Henry I. in 1135, "for every man that could forthwith robbed another." But when Edward I. succeeded to the throne in November, 1272, he was away on the crusade, and the prospect of a winter's interregnum was intolerable. Not only criminal justice, but all the comparatively recent forms of action which supposed a breach of the King's peace, would have been paralyzed; and, among others, the writ of trespass, fast becoming a popular remedy. The King's Council took on themselves to proclaim his peace forthwith, saying in his name: "for rendering justice and keeping of the peace we are now and henceforth"—not only after coronation—"debtors to all and sundry folk of this realm." It must have seemed a bold saying and a bold deed; but the wisdom of the new rule was so manifest that it was accepted as a conclusive precedent. We hear no more of the King's peace being suspended by the King's death, though several minor inconveniences of the same kind were allowed to persist, with no better justification, almost down to our own time. The later fiction of the Crown being a corporation sole was as useless as it is inelegant. Such an advanced doctrine as the personification of the State was (I need hardly say) quite beyond the scope of medieval lawyers, and indeed we are still, in England, without any apt words to express it in a legal form. In the United States it is much easier to perceive the true relations. Nevertheless the real working rule, even in England, is that the State is a corporate body of which the King and his constitutional advisers are the managing directors.

For the immediate purpose, however, it is enough that there is always a King and he is always bound to keep the peace of the realm. Justices of the peace (as we say now, but the commoner form was "of peace" down to the eighteenth century) are the King's officers appointed to see to the performance of this royal office in their respective counties. The long and complex chain of statutory authority which has defined their powers and duties goes back to the fourteenth century; but before the end of the twelfth century there were knights assigned to take the oaths of all lawful men for the maintenance of the peace. There is some ground to think that Simon de Montfort, during his short tenure of power, intended to use these earlier conservators of the peace as a check on the sheriffs. Indeed the King appears to have done the like already, though with different objects. Be that as it may, our English justices of the peace have at most times been less official persons and less subject to what we now call bureaucratic influence than any other royal officers in the world. Their judgments have not been always free from the bias of class and education, but they have also not been dictated by superiors. Down to the Restoration and later they combined the functions of subordinate judges with those of public prosecutors, and in their mixed executive and judicial capacity they did not escape the inquisitorial bent of Tudor administration and legislation. For some time we were near having a preliminary criminal procedure not unlike that of modern French law. But our modern police organization and Summary Jurisdiction Acts have completely restored the Common Law standard. The committing magistrate's court is now as open and judicial as the Court of Quarter Sessions or the superior courts themselves. Justices of the peace have naturally not contributed much to the direct development of the law, save so far as their action has been judicially confirmed or corrected in reported cases; they are not collectively a learned or professional body, though in fact they include many learned persons, and this makes them all the more useful as a link between the profession and the general public. The modern stipendiary magistrate is a specialized and salaried justice of the peace, in somewhat the same fashion as the modern policeman is a specialized and salaried constable with additional duties and powers. With this exception, the multifarious work of justices is unpaid. The constant additions made to it by legislation down to our own time are sufficient proof that on the whole, in spite of occasional miscarriages and current jests about "justices' justice," the country is content with the manner in which it is done.

We have seen royal authority and privilege break down ancient formalism only to become themselves the new instruments of the vital national ideals whose old instruments were unmanageable. We may see a combination, as it seems, of formalism and of privilege giving our superior courts the largest immunities and powers of self-help, deliberately confirmed by modern policy. Judges cannot be sued, as we all know, for anything done or said by them in their judicial capacity; the only difference between superior and inferior courts for this purpose is that the acts of a superior court are presumed to have been within its jurisdiction, while in the case of an inferior court the competence must be proved. The law is well settled by abundant modern authority. This is an exceptional rule, for the mere fact that the judge is doing the King's business is, I need hardly say, no defence at all against a plaintiff entitled to be protected by the law of the land. The general principle is that the sheriff, for example, must find and take the right man's goods at his peril. Why are the discretion and motives of a judge not examinable? I suggest, with some diffidence, for I know of no clear early authorities, that our special rule was in the first instance due to survival of the archaic feeling that a kind of sanctity attaches to judicial acts once completed. This was reinforced by the later but still archaic reverence of the early Middle Ages for the sanctity of authentic writing, and took the technical form of holding that ordinary methods of litigation and proof could not be admitted to falsify the record of the court. Coke did talk of the eminent position of the judges as the King's personal delegates to perform the duty of doing justice undertaken by his coronation oath; but the "sublimity" of the record appears to have chiefly weighed with him.

It was possible, indeed, down to the thirteenth century, to challenge the suitors of a popular court, or the lord of a private court, for false judgment. In the Anglo-Norman time the determination was by battle: *inde perveniri potuit ad duellum.* Convicted suitors might become infamous, the lord might lose his franchise; the judgment itself was untouched. The proceeding against jurors by attaint, which was in part statutory but was already obsolete in the practice of the sixteenth century, may perhaps be reckoned an offshoot of the same stock. All this, however, was superseded by the more effectual controlling powers of the superior courts. In the superior courts themselves means were found of correcting error and irregularity, though not on any complete or symmetrical plan. New judges had arisen in the land, who were not open to the old method of personal challenge; and, so far from any new personal remedy being provided (*a*), adventurous disappointed suitors who attempt to bring actions against judges have been thoroughly rebuffed in our modern practice. Experience shows, indeed, that in England at any rate such actions are devoid of merits and almost always merely vexatious. But the disallowance of them rests on the wider policy of maintaining to the full, and even exalting, the independence of the judicial power, and it is supported on that ground in all the modern authorities.

Not only have we given our courts an impregnable defensive position; we have put an offensive arm in their hands to deal swiftly and sharply with attempts to pervert the course of justice. Contempt of court was originally, no doubt, an offence fit for summary punishment because the court was the King's court, and to contemn it was to contemn the King. Indeed the Court of Chancery had originally no other sanction at all to enforce its process (*b*). Instead of the prosaic *alias* and *pluries* of the common law

(*a*) Such remedies were granted in the special cases of a judge refusing to issue a writ of *habeas corpus* or to sign a bill of exceptions. These cases, however, are abnormal.

(*b*) Blackst. iv. 287.

jurisdiction, it launched a writ of rebellion at contumacious defendants. The absolute power of committal for contempt is among the distinctive marks of a superior court; it was vindicated for justices of assize by the late Mr. Justice Willes in his memorable judgment in *Re Fernandez* (*a*), which, as I have already had occasion to note, is still the classical authority for the whole history of their office. At this day it is maintained on high general grounds of policy without regard to its origin. It is not my business here to consider whether it was wholly safe or wise to put such a weapon, unguarded by any kind of restriction, in the hands of persons exercising judicial authority in remote jurisdictions beyond seas where there is no effective professional or public opinion.

The war power known by the name, not a wholly fitting one in my opinion, of martial law was brought into renewed prominence by the recent troubles in South Africa. This is not the place to discuss the differences of opinion which still exist as to its precise extent. It is not likely that we shall ever have an authentic solution of them, as in practice an Act of Indemnity is always passed by the local legislature for the express purpose of covering doubtful cases. But I conceive it is the better opinion that the law of England, born and nurtured in times when war within the realm was very possible, is not without resources in the face of rebels and public enemies; that a right arising from and commensurate with the necessity is a part, though an extraordinary part, of the Common Law; that, though commonly and properly put in action by persons having executive authority, it is not in itself military or official, but is

(*a*) (1861), 10 C. B. N. S. 3.

an extension of the King's duty to preserve the peace, and of all citizens to aid in preserving it; and that, apart from statutory indemnities, the justification for acts done in this behalf is a common-law justification, and is accordingly examinable, after the restoration of peace, in the ordinary course of justice. It would be strange if private self-defence, even to extremity in certain cases, were justifiable, and the law and the public peace themselves were legally defenceless against enemies within the jurisdiction. The doctrine of the Crown having any prerogative in this matter, except so far as the duty of keeping the peace is specially incumbent on the King and his officers, appears to be needless in itself, and contrary to the principles of the Common Law. The opposite extreme doctrine that all acts, however necessary and proper in themselves, done in the name of so-called martial law must be illegal, and can be legalized only by an Act of Indemnity, seems contrary to common sense. And this, in the absence of decisive specific authority, amounts to saying that it is also contrary to the Common Law. But the general relation of our law to common sense, reason, or natural justice—for we may use any of these or other like terms at will—is a much larger subject, of which we shall next have to speak.

IV. The Law of Reason.

A. The Law of Nature and of Nations.

If there is one virtue that our books of authority claim for the Common Law more positively than another, it is that of being reasonable. The law is even said to be the perfection of reason. Not that the meaning of that saying is exhausted by the construction which a layman would naturally put upon it. For, as Coke had to tell King James I., much to his displeasure, there is an artificial reason of the law. Certainty is among the first objects of systematic justice. General principles being once fixed, the only way to attain certainty is to work out and accept their consequences, unless there is some very strong reason to the contrary. In hundreds of cases it is possible to suggest several rules of which, at first sight, any one would serve as well as another; and if we are asked why we have chosen one and rejected the others the answer is that the one we have preferred is deducible from our larger established principles, or at least consistent with and analogous to them, and the others are not. It is not good to choke rules with exceptions, merely for the sake of some small apparent convenience in the result, and at the risk of finding later that the exception, if not qualified by a second order of exceptions, is on the whole, less just than the rule. The sound method, as Parke laid down in an opinion given to the House of Lords seventy years ago, is to apply the settled rules of the law, where the application is not plainly unreasonable or inconvenient, to all cases which arise. But this very dictum assumes the existence, besides the reason which guides us in fixing the letter of the law, of a larger reason which informs the spirit of the law, and must, in the last resort, be the justification of the controlling rules themselves. Of this primary reason, too, not only book learning but every day's practice has much to tell us. Reasonable price and reasonable time are among the most familiar elements in our law of contract. Oftentimes no more definite instruction can be given to a jury than to award reasonable damages. "Natural reason and the just construction of the law," as Blackstone said, have given us the various applications of the common counts, extending to the whole field of what we now call Quasi-contract. In Lord Mansfield's hands the principles of natural equity were an enchanter's wand to call a whole new world of justice into being. The test of what a reasonable man's conduct would be in the circumstances governs our modern law of negligence and underlies those branches of it which have been specialized into groups of definite rules. Almost in our own time a simple and wholly untechnical conception of the same kind has been developed into the doctrine of estoppel "in pais," perhaps the most powerful and flexible instrument to be found in any system of civil jurisprudence. The scientific importance of this external standard of reasonableness, which enables the law to keep in close touch with the moral and practical sense of mankind in the affairs of life, was demonstrated once for all, more than twenty years ago, by my friend Mr. Justice Holmes; and if my own endeavours to pursue its application in detail have any value, it is largely due to his example.

What is the origin, and what are the doctrinal affinities, of this pervading ideal, of which it would be hardly too much to say that it is the life of the modern Common Law? It may seem paradoxical to answer that we owe it to the Greeks; and yet it goes near to be true. Christopher St. German, the very able and learned author of the "Doctor and Student," touched the right clue early in the sixteenth century. The Student of the laws of England, being asked by the Doctor of Divinity what he has to say of the Law of Nature, makes answer that among common lawyers the term is not in use, but they speak of reason where a canonist or civilian would speak of the Law of Nature. "It is not used among them that be learned in the laws of England, to reason what thing is commanded or prohibited by the Law of Nature, and what not, but all the reasoning in that behalf is under this manner. As when anything is grounded upon the Law of Nature, they say that Reason will that such a thing be done; and if it be prohibited by the Law of Nature, they say it is against Reason, or that Reason will not suffer that to be done" (*a*). It is curious that this passage should have been, so far as I know, completely overlooked; but the medieval tradition of the Law of Nature was broken up by the controversies of the Reformation, and seventeenth century writers are quite confused about it. This, however, does not alter the reality of the parallel as it stood in the sixteenth century, nor diminish the probability of a real connection with the

(*a*) Doct. and St. Dial. 1, c. 5.

scholastic doctrine, which was as much philosophical and political as legal. That doctrine rested partly on the Aristotelian distinction between natural and conventional justice, partly on the Latin expositions by Cicero and others of the same distinction as developed by the later Greek schools, and partly on the technical adaptation of it by the classical Roman jurists, who identified *lex naturalis* or *jus naturale* with the *jus gentium* of the Praetorian law, subject to one or two theoretical exceptions, which we have not to consider here. Directly or indirectly, therefore, the Law of Nature, as accepted throughout the Middle Ages, was derived from Greek theories of ethics (*a*).

Now the term *jus naturae*, not in use among English lawyers in St. German's time, does occur in our books, though not frequently, from the seventeenth to the nineteenth century, and we have a recent judicial interpretation of it. "The foundation of the right" [to water courses], says Farwell, J., "as stated throughout all the cases is *jus naturae*. . . . . I have come to the conclusion that *jus naturae* is used in these cases as expressing that principle in English law which is akin to, if not derived from, the *jus naturale* of Roman law. English law is, of course, quite independent of Roman law, but the conception of *aequum et bonum*, and the rights flowing therefrom which are included in *jus naturale* underlie a great part of English Common Law; although it is not usual to find 'the law of nature' or 'natural law' referred to in so many words in English cases. . . . . I am not, therefore, introducing any novel principle if I regard *jus naturae*, on which the right to running water rests, as meaning that

(*a*) See Journ. Soc. Comp. Legisl. 1900, p. 418 *sqq.*

which is *aequum et bonum* between the upper and lower proprietors " (*a*).

The Roman conception involved in "*aequum et bonum*" or "*aequitas*" is identical with what we mean by "reasonable," or very nearly so. Such has been the result obtained, in modern times, by the application of historical scholarship to the Roman authorities on their own ground. On the whole, the natural justice or "reason of the thing" which the Common Law recognizes and applies does not appear to differ from the law of nature which the Romans identified with *jus gentium* and the medieval doctors of canon and civil law boldly adopted as being divine law revealed through man's natural reason. I do not assume that our Germanic customary law, set free from the fetters of its original archaic procedure, was not capable of striking out an equivalent guiding principle for itself. But we have to remember that the whole of medieval thought was pervaded by a craving for authority, or at least a plausible show of it. Best of all was the text of scripture, whether taken in the natural sense or not. Aristotle was next best. Cicero was very well. Ovid, or Virgil, or almost any Roman author, was well enough in the absence of any more commanding name. Is it too fanciful to connect this habit of mind with the deeply rooted Germanic custom of vouching a warrantor? I know not; but it is certain that the medieval author who had nobody to vouch appeared to his contemporaries either to display indecent arrogance or to confess discreditable ignorance. In the present case the Law of Nature was there; not merely a doctrine or rule of the imperial law,

(*a*) *Bradford Corporation* v. *Ferrand,* [1902] 2 Ch. 655, 661.

to which English lawyers could not be openly beholden, but a principle sanctioned by the Church as fundamental and paramount. The Roman lawyers, in search of a rational sanction for the authority of the *jus gentium*, had gone to the Greek philosophy of natural justice; the medieval publicists, twelve centuries later, found in their revived learning this fabric of natural reason claiming respect by the triple authority of Aristotle, Cicero, and the Corpus Juris; this last, be it observed, being no pagan document, but the legislation of the orthodox emperor Justinian. Evidently the Law of Nature must have its place in the Christian system of Church and State, and no mean place. The problem was solved in the Decretum of Gratian by identifying the Law of Nature with the Law of God, as the Roman jurists had identified the *jus gentium* with the Law of Nature. According to the canonical doctors, the law revealed to man in natural reason is no less truly revealed and no less divine than any specific precept of scripture; it is of paramount and universal obligation, and no positive precept of any law, human or divine, can be set up against it. If any specific revelation appears to contradict the Law of Nature, it must have been wrongly interpreted.

Our founders of the thirteenth century, Raleigh, and Pateshull, and Henry of Bratton, were themselves ecclesiastics. They were more or less learned in the Canon Law; they must have known what the professed canonists were doing. It is not credible that a doctrine which pervaded all political speculation in Europe, and was assumed as a common ground of authority by the opposing champions of the Empire and the Papacy, should have been without influence among learned men in England. If it be asked why the sages of the Common Law did not expressly refer to the Law of Nature, the answer is that at no time after, at latest, the Papal interference in the English politics of the first half of the thirteenth century, was the citation of Roman canonical authority acceptable in our country, save so far as it was necessary for strictly technical purposes. Besides, any such citation might have been construed as a renunciation of independence, or a submission of questions of general policy to the judgment of the Church. These considerations appear sufficient to explain why "it is not used among them that be learned in the laws of England to reason what thing is commanded or prohibited by the Law of Nature."

Since the Middle Ages the Law of Nature, or of Reason, besides its distinct manifestations in foreign systems, has been a principal or influential factor in developing the following branches of jurisprudence: Equity, the Law Merchant, the Law of Nations, the general application, within the sphere of municipal law, of the principles of natural justice and reasonableness, and the body of rules for the choice of law and jurisdiction, and the application of foreign law, which we sum up under the head of Conflict of Laws or Private International Law. These are all of frequent importance in our daily practice. It is becoming less and less possible for the man who would be an accomplished lawyer to neglect any of them. We are now concerned not to trace the leading principles into their various consequences, which is the office of special treatises, but to observe how the Common Law has not only adopted but assimilated them, and has thereby enriched its resources for doing justice without losing anything of its individual character. It was with our law as with a young commonwealth growing in wealth and strength. At first we lived in fear of surprises and usurpations; we were suspicious of foreign influence, not because it might be bad, but because it was foreign; we were jealously insular and held strangers at arm's length. When we had assured our existence and independence, we opened our gates. We welcomed new settlers with their arts and industries; we became willing and eager to make their accomplishments our own. But we held fast to our national genius, and gave our fullest welcome to those who would enter into our national life no longer as strangers, but as citizens. Natural justice is good for the emergencies of unsettled times and extraordinary occasions, but precarious. It is made a permanent possession, secured against caprice and degeneration, only when it is embodied in legal justice.

Equity, as is well known, grew out of the king's special authority and duty to supplement the defects of the ordinary law and reinforce the weakness of its procedure. The early Chancellors did not disclose the sources of their inspiration; probably they had as good grounds of expediency for not talking about the Law of Nature as the common lawyers. Certainly they intended and endeavoured to follow the dictate of natural reason; and if their version of natural justice was somewhat artificial in its details, and bore a decided civilian or canonical stamp, this was only to be expected. Some centuries later, when British judicial officers in India were instructed to decide, in the absence of any native law applicable to both parties, according to "justice, equity, and good conscience," the results bore, even more manifestly, the stamp of the Common Law. But of this we shall have to say a word later. The Court of Chancery, having passed through its early stage of doing battle with obstinate oppressors of the poor and deniers of right, found itself charged, by means of its jurisdiction over trusts, with the administration of estates and the adjustment of intricate conflicting claims to property. Valiant in the cause of good conscience, the court made the attempt to attain perfect justice, and, lest any form of fraud should escape, spread its nets with infinite ingenuity. Some of you may remember the terribly multifarious contents of the heading "Constructive Fraud" in the old-fashioned books on equity. Logically, nothing could be less defensible than such a catalogue, or more bewildering to young students. Thirty years ago I was so bewildered, at any rate, that I could see no way out of the tangle unless I cleared my head by writing a book myself—and I did. Historically, this jumble of diverse matters did more or less faithfully represent an actual process. A's conduct, let us say, is admitted to be fraudulent, and fit to be restrained by the court. B's conduct is rather like A's, and C's is rather like B's; therefore let B and C be restrained, though fraud cannot be proved. So was natural reason driven to work by sap and mine rather than by direct attack, the leaders of the Common Law not being yet bold enough to aid it openly. The court's operations, carried out under these conditions, were too much apart from common understanding, and ran into excessive refinement. The natural reason of just men was overlaid with elaborate artifices, and safeguards were multiplied at a cost out of all proportion to the substance of what was to be preserved. It was forgotten that a fairly good working decision rendered within a moderate time is better than an ideal decision postponed for an indefinite time, and that decisions which are to be respected by the community at large should be intelligible as well as just. Not content with requiring integrity, the court sought to impose a standard of prudence and vigilance beyond the powers of ordinary mortals, and barely compatible with the ordinary conduct of business. Thus, with the best intentions, it deposed the reasonable man of the Common Law or the *bonus paterfamilias* of the Civil Law to set up a monster of impossible caution, and put many really innocent persons in situations of great hardship. More than once in recent times legislation was found necessary to abolish or mitigate these inconveniences. In England the fusion of legal and equitable jurisdiction under the Judicature Acts since 1875, worked out in the judgments of a single Court of Appeal wielding comprehensive powers and including judges trained in both systems, has saved our equity jurisprudence, not too soon, from being righteous overmuch. Conscientiousness is good; the standard of the Common Law itself is in many respects higher than what commonly passes muster among men of good business repute, and it would be disastrous if it were lowered. Still the conscience of the court, if it is to be an effective power, must not run away from the common sense of mankind.

Perhaps the best example of the sound and legitimate work of equity, proceeding on broad principles of justice and convenience, and giving permanent definition to reasonable practice tried by long experience, is to be found in the law of partnership. That law is modern and self-contained; it owes very little to early precedents and hardly anything to legislation; in about a century it grew to a condition so settled and so acceptable as to be ripe for codification. In 1890 it was codified in England, and no material fault has been found with the result. The commissioners on uniformity of legislation who have already done so much excellent work in the United States are now turning their attention to the same subject, and it may not be many years before we see a substantially identical law of partnership enacted for the English-speaking world; enacted as was the Negotiable Instruments Law, not by the invention of any one man or generation, but on the firm base of the combined legal and commercial reason of several generations.

The Law Merchant, as it existed through the Middle Ages, was undoubtedly a body of cosmopolitan custom, resting its claim to allegiance not on any express reception by municipal authority, but on its intrinsic reasonableness evidenced by the general consent and usage of the persons concerned. It was recognized and constantly described as being part of the Law of Nature. Thus Sir John Davies, writing in the first quarter of the seventeenth century, said: "The Law Merchant, as it is a part of the law of nature and nations, is universal and one and the same in all countries in the world." Much earlier, in 1473, in the celebrated case of the fraudulent carrier which is the ultimate authority for the doctrine of larceny by breaking bulk, Bishop Stillington, Edward IV.'s Chancellor, had laid down that suits between merchant strangers ought to be determined by the law of nature in the Chancery. The king has jurisdiction by the fact of the stranger's coming into the realm, but he must exercise it according to the law of nature which some call the Law Merchant, and which is universal throughout the world. We learn from

Malines (*a*), in his *Lex Mercatoria*, that in practice the Chancellor referred such causes to be determined by a commission of merchants, and that this did not conduce to expedition. Meanwhile the Common Law had gone very near to recognizing the custom of merchants, it would seem rather as a kind of personal law than on any more general ground. We have two examples in the late Year Books of Edward I. of suits between merchants being pleaded in the king's courts according to the law merchant (*b*). It does not appear why this practice was discontinued. Later we find allegations of local customs which look very much as if they were part of the general Law Merchant, and were pleaded in that special form only to compel the court to take notice of them (*b*).

Perhaps it was as well that the reception of the Law Merchant into the Common Law was deferred until it could be received deliberately and in a mature form. In the eighteenth century the law of nature had been recast by Grotius and his successors in a shape fitted for modern use, and without prejudice to its permanently valuable elements. The adoption of the Law Merchant, under the directing genius of Lord Mansfield, was really a development of the same process, as was also the introduction of equitable methods into our ordinary legal procedure through the machinery of the common counts. No further comment on Lord Mansfield's work is called for here; it is as well known as anything in the history of our law, and its praise is recorded in judgments which are themselves

(*a*) So he signs his preface: he is Malynes on the title-page.

(*b*) References in "The History of the Law of Nature," Journ. Soc. Comp. Legisl. 1900, p. 431; Pollock, Principles of Contract, 7th ed. p. 141.

classical. But it is important to observe that the Law Merchant was not incorporated into our system, as some have contended, as a fixed body of rules incapable of addition. It is still in fact a living body of custom, and English decisions have quite lately recognized this fact. We now hold that a new general mercantile usage may be proved, and that, once proved, the courts will thenceforth take judicial notice of it. On the other hand, as there is a complete incorporation of the Law Merchant in the Common Law, so there must be a certain conformity. The Law Merchant is not a foreign law, or the custom of a particular class, to be recognized and applied, in substitution of the Common Law, in appropriate circumstances; it is an integral part of our law itself. Therefore the settled principles applicable to men's ordinary affairs cannot be displaced, or settled forms dispensed with, merely for the supposed convenience of business. The seventeenth section of the Statute of Frauds may be a wise enactment or not; but we are not free to disregard it in a court of justice because it is the custom of a particular trade to rely on bare spoken words or unsigned notes. Lord Mansfield himself endeavoured to reduce the requirement of consideration for informal contracts to a mere rule of evidence inapplicable to commercial transactions in writing, but the attempt was unsuccessful. It is useless to speculate on what might have happened if there could have been a Lord Mansfield in the fifteenth century. The Law Merchant has had to pay something for the rights of full citizenship, but the price was moderate and inevitable.

The history of the other great cosmopolitan offshoot of the Law of Nature, namely international law, is not within our present scope. But I cannot refrain from pointing out the fallacy of one reason confidently given by English jurists of the so-called analytical school, any time during the last half century, for not allowing the law of nations to be truly law at all. It is said that a system of rules cannot be law when it lacks the sanction of a tribunal and of regular decisions: and the view that international law depends merely on convention (which Lord Stowell declared to be fit only for Barbary pirates) may be found not only in text books, but in reported judgments given in cases of great importance. I do not admit the validity of the argument, if the fact were as alleged; but the supposed fact is in truth subject to large exceptions. Not only international questions of allegiance and territorial jurisdiction, of the existence and consequences of war between foreign powers (whether officially recognized as sovereign states or not), of blockade and its incidents, and the like, may be and frequently have been the subjects of decision in municipal courts; but a material part of the law of war, namely the law of prize, has been administered, and still may be, by courts of admiralty, and expressly as an international and not as a local law. Prize courts administer the law of nations and have never purported to administer anything else. "The seat of judicial authority is locally here, in the belligerent country, according to the known law and practice of nations, but the law itself has no locality." This is only a sample of Lord Stowell's utterances. No doubt is possible that he conceived himself to be administering a law that was *jus gentium* in the fullest sense, a rule not of local but of universal obligation. The same view has been consistently held and applied in the Supreme Court of the United States; I should rather think, indeed, that American jurists regard it as elementary. Thus although it is true that for some parts of the law of nations there is at present no tribunal, or none with coercive jurisdiction, it is equally true that a considerable part of it is actually within the sphere of positive jurisprudence.

In our system the Law of Nature has formally retreated from one untenable position; but the position, as we shall immediately see, had never been effectively occupied. It was a current opinion among the medieval doctors that rules of positive municipal law were controlled by the law of nature, and not binding if they were contrary to it; though some advocates of the Emperor's independent authority in secular matters, as against the claim of universal supremacy for the Pope, avoided inconvenient consequences by tempering the general proposition with a rather strong presumption that the acts of the lawful sovereign were right. Opposition to princes and rulers in vindication of the law of nature was possible, but at the opposer's peril if he were mistaken, and not to be lightly entered upon. So limited, this natural right can hardly be distinguished from the ultimate moral right, admitted by all modern publicists, of resisting an intolerably bad government. However, the doctrine without its politic qualification found an echo in England, where the king's judges always looked on legislative interference with some jealousy—a jealousy too often warranted by the unworkmanlike manner in which Parliament has laid hands on the Common Law. We find a series of dicta, extending to the early part of the eighteenth century, to the effect that statutes contrary to "natural justice" or "common right" may be treated as void. This opinion is most strongly expressed by Coke, but, like many of his confident opinions, is extra-judicial. Although Coke was no canonist, we may be pretty sure that it was ultimately derived from the canonist doctrine prevailing on the Continent of Europe. In England it was never a practical doctrine. The nearest approach to real authority for it is a case of the 27th year of Henry VI., known to us only through Fitzherbert's Abridgment, where the court held an Act of Parliament to be inoperative, not because it was contrary to natural justice, but because they could make no sense of it at all. Sir Thomas More, after the verdict against him for a novel statutory treason, and before judgment, objected that "this indictment is grounded upon an Act of Parliament directly repugnant to the laws of God and his Holy Church," and "is therefore in law, among Christian men, insufficient to charge any Christian man." The objection was disregarded without being expressly overruled. It is easy to understand why Elizabethan lawyers refrained from adducing this example. At this day the courts have expressly disclaimed any power to control an Act of Parliament. Blackstone characteristically talks in the ornamental part of his introduction about the law of nature being supreme and, when he comes to particulars, asserts the uncontrollable power of Parliament in the most explicit terms, following herein Sir Thomas Smith, a civilian whose political insight was much greater than that of the common lawyers of his time. It hardly needs to be pointed out that, in states where there is a distinction between a written constitution, or fundamental constitutional laws however called, and ordinary legislation, the question whether any particular act of the legislature is or is not in accordance with the Constitution depends not on any general views of natural justice, but on the interpretation of the constitutional provisions which are the supreme law of the land. But I may remind you in passing that such a distinction, while it is necessary in a federal constitution, is also quite possible in a state having a single centralized government, and exists at this day in a majority of the civilized commonwealths of the world. The omnipotence of the British Parliament, on which English jurists have been too apt to build their theories of sovereignty and legislation, is really exceptional. On its own ground, however, it is established beyond any doubt.

B. Natural Justice in the Common Law.

The real and fruitful conquests of the principle of natural justice or reasonableness in our law belong to its modern growth. Students fresh from striving with the verbal archaism of our law-books must find it hard to realize that the nineteenth century, after the thirteenth, has been the most vital period of the Common Law. The greater part of our actual working jurisprudence was made by men born in the early years of that century, the contemporaries of Darwin and Emerson. A hundred years ago the law of contract was, to say the least, very far from complete, and the law of negligence and all cognate subjects was rudimentary. No such proposition could then have been enunciated as that every lawful man is bound (exceptions excepted) to use in all his doings the care and caution, at least, of a man of average prudence to avoid causing harm to his neighbours, and is entitled in turn to presume that they will use reasonable care both for him and for themselves. Now it has become a commonplace, and the wayfarer who reads, as he approaches a railroad crossing, the brief words of warning, "Stop, look, listen," little thinks that they sum up a whole history of keen discussion. The standard of a reasonable man's conduct has been taken by courts from the verdicts of juries, and consolidated into judicial rules; and we have a body of authority covering all the usual occasions of men's business and traffic, and already tending to be, if anything, too elaborate. All this owes very little indeed to early precedents. The medieval feeling seems to have been rather that, outside a few special and stringent rules, a man should be held liable only for default in what he had positively undertaken; and, in days when mechanical arts were few and simple, and the determination of disputed facts was still a rude and uncertain process, this may have served well enough. But the law was capable of growing to the demands of new times and circumstances; its conclusions in detail were not dogmas, but flexible applications of living and still expanding principles. The knowledge and resources of a reasonable man are far greater in the twentieth than in the sixteenth or the eighteenth century, and accordingly so much the more is required of him. A defendant must clear himself by showing, not that he acted to the best of his own judgment, or with a degree of prudence that would have been sufficient in the Middle Ages, but that his action was such as is to be expected here and now from a man competent so far as any special competence was required in the business he was about, and otherwise not below the general standard of a capable citizen's information, intelligence, and caution. A plaintiff, on the other hand, is not free to neglect obvious opportunities of avoiding harm, though the defendant's negligence may have put him in danger in the first instance. He must not charge the defendant with consequences which he himself had the means of averting, and could finally have averted by the exercise of ordinary prudence. This is, broadly stated, the doctrine of contributory negligence, a doctrine in no way formal or technical, notwithstanding ingenious attempts to make it so, and founded solely on general principles of reason and convenience, and on the inherent power of the Common Law to mould its rules in accordance with those principles as the habits of men's life are modified by new inventions, and new cases, produced by such modifications, arise for determination. It may be supported by the analogy, so far as that goes, of some opinions of the classical Roman lawyers in their interpretations of the *lex Aquilia*, themselves resting on like grounds of natural reason; but its growth has been quite independent.

Even more remarkable is the formation, dating from less than forty years ago (though one or two eminent judges threw out hints of it earlier), of a rule or body of rules demanding a special and intensified caution from the occupiers of what we call, for this purpose, fixed property. The term is not quite adequate for some of the later developments of the doctrine, but is sufficiently understood. I have ventured to group these rules, which are still increasing in importance, under the rubric of "Duties of Insuring Safety." The justification of their existence lies not in any ancient maxims or forms of pleading, but in the intrinsic and indefeasible competence of the law to stand in the forefront of social morality. We have powers of controlling the material world, and holding its various energies ready to be directed to our ends, which were wholly unknown to our forefathers. With those powers have come risks which were equally unknown to them. Going beyond the letter of their books, we have extended the old remedies to meet those risks; and yet we are faithful to the spirit of the medieval sages, and something more, for we have called in the archaic strictness of the law of trespass to give a hand to the deliberate exigency of our modern policy.

Probably there was nothing in the early rules of cattle trespass and the like more politic or subtle than the common archaic assumption that a given set of external facts, if they do not make a man liable conclusively and without qualification, will not make him liable at all. In following and enlarging such rules we have really set them on a new foundation. Responsibility to one's neighbours increases in proportion as one's undertaking involves elements of common danger; and there comes a point of risk at which nothing short of "consummate care" will serve, and no prudence is allowed to count as such in law which has not proved sufficient to avert disaster in fact. It is not for me to discuss here whether the Common Law, in the jurisdictions which accept this last doctrine—for it is not everywhere accepted—has not been tempted into an excess of zeal against negligence, as Equity once was against fraud. The zeal that devours is better, at any rate, than sloth that rusts. There must be fluctuations and now and then a false step in a secular process like that of our science. We think no less of the achievements of great masters in the graphic arts because they reveal to the curious eye little slips of the tool or of the brush, the traces of a changed purpose or a corrected execution which are technically known as *pentimenti*. And a living system of law must be judged not only as a science but as an art.

More direct and avowed applications of natural justice are not wanting. Powers of a judicial nature are frequently exercised by governing bodies of various kinds, trustees of public institutions, directors of companies, committees of clubs, and the like, who have a statutory or conventional authority over their officers and members, and are invested with the duty of hearing and determining complaints of misconduct. Dismissal from an office of profit, or deprivation of membership and its incidental rights in corporate or quasi-corporate property, may be the result. From such decisions the court will not entertain an appeal on the general merits. But it will not allow the rules of universal justice to be disregarded. Whatever forms are prescribed in the particular case must be observed; the person charged with misconduct must not be condemned without adequate notice and an adequate opportunity of being heard; and the decision must be rendered in good faith for the interest of the society or institution whose authority is being exercised. Exceptionally, for reasons of policy, there may be an absolute as distinguished from a judicial discretion, a purposely unlimited power to dismiss or deprive without giving any reason at all. Such a power must be expressly conferred by legislation or by the terms of a contract to which the person to be affected is a party. There may be very good cause for its existence; but such express provisions, when they exist, do not impeach the validity of the general principle.

There is a much more delicate question somewhat analogous to this, namely whether a municipal court can disregard the judgment of a foreign court of competent jurisdiction merely on the ground that the result is manifestly contrary to natural justice. On the whole the acceptable opinion would seem to be that such a power exists, but that it is a reserved power to be exercised only with the greatest caution and in an extreme case. We have learned to say that the verdict of a jury will not be set aside merely because the court does not agree with it, but only if it appears to be such as no reasonable jury could have arrived at upon the evidence. The judgment of a foreign court acting within its jurisdiction must be entitled to as much respect.

I have endeavoured to show that the Law of Nature is not, as the English utilitarians in their ignorance of its history supposed, a synonym for arbitrary individual preference, but that on the contrary it is a living embodiment of the collective reason of civilized mankind, and as such is adopted by the Common Law in substance though not always by name. But it has its limits; they are pointed out in the very earliest Aristotelian exposition, and it must be admitted that attempts to overstep them have sometimes led to failure. Natural justice has no means of fixing any rule to terms defined in number or measure, nor of choosing one practical solution out of two or more which are in themselves equally plausible. Positive law, whether enacted or customary, must come to our aid in such matters. It would be no great feat for natural reason to tell us that a rule of the road is desirable; but it could never have told us whether to drive to the right hand or to the left, and in fact custom has settled this differently in different countries, and even, in some parts of Europe, in different provinces of one State.

In the eighteenth century a bold and ingenious attempt was made in England to establish copyright at Common Law by arguments drawn from the Law of Nature; and it seemed to be on the point of success. For a time the weight of opinion was in its favour. But such a right, if it existed, could not be limited in time; it must be perpetual if it was anything extending beyond the author's lifetime. An argument might perhaps be framed for a right exerciseable only by the author in person, and therefore co-extensive with his life; but this would not have satisfied authors. Plausible reasons for what is called "property in ideas" were certainly forthcoming; they are still sometimes urged by men of letters and lay publicists. But in a later generation the tide of legal opinion had turned. In the middle of the nineteenth century both sides were ably supported among the judges, but the House of Lords was unanimous (though actual decision of the point was not called for) against the existence of the alleged right; and this on grounds of general reason and convenience—in other words, of natural justice. It may be doubted whether the law of nature be competent in any case, within or even outside the bounds of the Common Law, to invent definite new forms of property. But, however that may be, general consent is the only practical warrant for the adoption of any suggested rule as being dictated by universal justice; and here the only general consent which could be inferred from the conflict of opinions was a consensus that authors ought to have some kind of reasonable security for enjoying the fruit of their labour. The question what the kind and amount of protection shall be, when once a limited protection is admitted in principle, can only stand remitted to legislation; and that way has in fact been taken everywhere. The problem is now not to find a philosophic basis, but to get the copyright laws of civilized countries reduced to tolerable simplicity, and brought, if possible, to an approximate uniformity. There is an antecedent right to restrain the publication of unpublished matter, often erroneously called copyright before publication, and sometimes treated as an incident of property, sometimes as arising from a presumed contract or term of a contract. This does appear to rest, in the last analysis, on considerations of natural justice more than on any satisfying deduction from positive ownership or obligation. Of this class of rights not much can be said with confidence at present. It is being slowly developed by occasional decisions, but, so far as authority goes, it is neither well defined nor adequately explained, and does not seem likely to be so for several years to come. One day the time will be ripe for clear light to be struck out from a leading judgment or series of judgments, and then a new chapter of natural reason will be added to our law, and we shall all wonder why so plain a rule was not understood sooner. The jurists of Continental Europe, not without provocation, consider our lawyers lamentably ignorant of natural law; some English writers, half a century behind their time, still maintain the obsolete Benthamite aversion to its name; meanwhile our courts have to go on making a great deal of law which is really natural law, whether they know it or not. For, as we said at the outset of these lectures, they must find a solution, with or without authority, for every case that comes before them: and general considerations of justice and convenience must be relied on in default of positive authority. There is no reason why they should not be openly invoked, for the alternative method of pretending to follow authority where there is really none is now discredited. These general considerations are nothing else than what our ancestors of the Middle Ages and the Renaissance understood by the Law of Nature. It is not within our province to show here how a term with a venerable history, and capable of perfectly rational application, came, after the disruption of the scholastic traditions, to be perverted and misconceived for nearly two centuries.

Just now there is a group of questions before courts of common law both in America and in England, arising out of the rapid modern development of trade combinations, which go to the very foundation of the law of personal liberty and of civil wrongs. Individuals, in our system of society, cannot effectually protect their common interests otherwise than by common organized action. But this very protective action, in itself legitimate, easily reaches a point where it creates powers liable to grave abuse, and, even without manifest abuse, bears hardly on dissentient individuals within the sphere of interest in question, on persons and classes having opposed interests, and, in possible and not infrequent cases, on the common weal at large. The problem is nothing less than to reconcile the just freedom of new kinds of collective action with the ancient and just independence of the individual citizen. It would be idle here to express any opinion upon the issues involved, or to attempt any forecast of the ultimate solution. Such an attempt would lead to a digression altogether disproportionate to the matter in hand, and still too brief to have any value of its own. This much is certain, that no merely technical resources of the law will suffice for the task. In whatever jurisdiction the decisive word is spoken, it will be founded on knowledge of the world, and on broad considerations of policy. Natural law will have, in other words, a large and probably a dominant part in it.

The Common Law, then, has largely enriched and is still enriching itself by associating the Law of Nature with its authority. The Law of Nature has in turn carried the spirit and much of the substance of the Common Law to regions where that law never claimed, or has even expressly disclaimed, formal jurisdiction. A professor of the Common Law set down in British India, without previous information, would find himself, on the whole, in the familiar atmosphere of his own law. He would observe that Asiatic suitors, living under customs intimately bound up with their religions, are judged by those customs in matters of religion, marriage and inheritance. Allowing for this exception, he would be prone to infer that the Common Law had at some time and in some way been received as governing civil relations in general. But in fact our courts in India do not profess, outside the limited statutory jurisdiction of the High Courts of the Presidency towns over European British subjects, to administer English law as such. In the early days of our trading settlements, European merchants were presumed, according to the universal custom of Asia, which was also the custom of merchant communities in Europe in the Middle Ages, to carry their own law with them. A charter of Charles II., due to the acquisition of Bombay, seems to have contemplated the establishment of a court or courts to administer the law merchant to traders. It does not appear that this provision came into effect: in any case the subsequent adoption of the law merchant by the Common Law superseded it. A century later, and on the other side of India, the East India Company's courts, in the territory which the company governed as the nominal delegate of the Mogul emperors, aimed at doing justice according to the native laws of the suitors. But the parties were often of different provinces, or religions, or both, not owing obedience to any common rule; and for many of the growing modern relations of business there was no rule at all to be found in any native law. This being so, a Bengal Regulation instructed the Company's courts in 1793 "to act according to justice, equity and good conscience"; and this, being followed in the same or like words by the other provincial Regulations, became the general rule of the Company's jurisdiction. In terms this amounted to a comprehensive enactment of the Law of Nature. Such would be its obvious meaning to any publicist down to the end of the eighteenth century. But the Law of Nature, as we have already noted, does not provide a detailed system for the guidance of municipal tribunals. It can tell us that men ought to keep faith and perform their contracts; it can no more tell us what are the requisites of a lawfully binding contract at Benares than what they are at Providence or at New Haven. English magistrates had to do the best justice they could, and the only justice they were familiar with was the justice of the Common Law. Thus, under the name of justice, equity, and good conscience, the general law of British India, save so far as the authority of native laws was preserved, came to be so much of English law as was considered applicable, or rather was not considered inapplicable, to the conditions of Indian society. At this day the reported decisions of the English courts are freely, perhaps too freely, cited by keen-witted native pleaders all over India, and relied on by Hindu and Mahometan judges of the Indian High Courts, of whom some would be worthy companions to any of our own chiefs. There are four independent jurisdictions in India whose decisions are reported (Allahabad, Bombay, Calcutta, and Madras); but an appeal lies from them all to the Judicial Committee of the Privy Council, and the divergences have not been very serious. All the High Courts endeavour, so far as consistent with local legislation, to keep abreast of the progress of English law at home. A somewhat analogous process took place in the Middle Ages, when, in the French provinces of customary law, the Roman law, though not received as binding, enjoyed a persuasive authority as being an embodiment of written reason, and impressed its own character on a formally independent jurisprudence.

Much of the Anglo-Indian law has been consolidated in codes within the last generation or thereabouts. This was not the imposition of new law by legislative authority, but, in intention at least, the affirmation of existing law and practice, with a certain number of specific amendments and the determination of a certain number of controverted points. I ought to mention, perhaps, that the history of criminal law in British India stands to some extent apart. The Company's courts attempted to administer Mahometan penal law, which they found in possession. But the experiment proved unsatisfactory, and after a variety of makeshifts and long delay, a Penal Code, being a simplified version of English Criminal Law, was enacted for British India in 1861. The original draft had been prepared many years earlier by a commission of which Macaulay was the leading member. The text bears his mark plainly enough, and the introductory minute is now part of his collected works. This was the earliest of the Anglo-Indian Codes, and has been the most successful. It is remarkable that our criminal law, notwithstanding its conspicuous defects of form, has almost everywhere prevailed over competing systems, even where the Common Law was not received as a whole. Witness the Province of Quebec, where the Civil Code represents the old French law of the colony, modified by free use of the Napoleonic Code and in some particulars by English influence, but the criminal law is the substantially English Criminal Code of the Dominion. The Indian Penal Code has itself become a centre of influence, and a model for more or less close imitation, not only among the native states of India (with whose domestic legislation the Government of India does not interfere, provided that the essentials of good government are respected), but in Ceylon, the Sudan, and some other territories under British dominion or protection.

It is curious to reflect, at this day, that a generation or two ago, when the internal expansion and the external conquests of the Common Law were in full tide, it was a prevalent opinion among thoughtful and learned persons in England that the judicial development of the law had seen its best days, and the sceptre had passed to legislation. Historical formulas about stages and periods may be useful servants; they must not be allowed to become masters. Very good of its kind, but still of that kind, is the maxim, originated, I believe, by Sir Henry Maine, that there is an age of fictions, an age of equity, and an age of legislation. The positive truth contained in it is of great value. Equity taken in a large sense, the free constructive development of law, consciously directed to ends of justice and convenience, is possible only when jurisprudence has become or is in the way of becoming a science. Again, the scale and importance of legislation in the world we now live in depend on the political conditions of modern society as a whole as well as on the existence of a formally competent legislature. But we have no right to make the negative or exclusive inference that equity, when it came in, left no room for fictions, and that legislation in turn has superseded equity. No such inference is warranted by the actual history of the law. One of the most brilliant and successful fictions of the Common Law, quite lately confirmed to the full in England by the House of Lords, is less than half a century old, I mean the implied warranty of authority which is attached to the acts of a professed agent. The activity of Equity, whether we take it in the artificial sense of the law and remedies formerly peculiar to the Court of Chancery, or in the wider sense just now mentioned, has not diminished but increased in the last generation. Legislation itself is to no small extent conditioned by the continuing evolution of professional jurisprudence. The law cannot afford to throw away any of its resources; we must hold fast to them all. Many are the books of practice, once in every lawyer's hands, that have had their day, and are stacked like the obsolete weapons of European armouries, a "dumb dread people,"—if I may pervert a phrase of Mr. Swinburne's—who sit forgotten on the upper shelves of Austin Hall and Lincoln's Inn. Forms of pleading and rules of procedure pass away like the matchlock and the pike; but our fundamental methods and traditions, like the principles of the art of war, do not pass away. Julius Cæsar would know what to do with a cyclist battalion, and Gustavus Adolphus would recognize his own ideas in the machine gun. Mahan expounds the strategy of the modern battle-ship in the names of Raleigh and Nelson. That earlier Raleigh who was Henry of Bratton's master would not be afraid to grapple with code pleading, and the judges who framed the Statute of Wales would not be behind John Marshall in building up a federal jurisdiction.

The old flag, the old watchwords, the old discipline, the latest knowledge and the newest arms—these are the approved instruments of victory in peace as in war. For whom is the next campaign of the law? For you to whom I speak, you who are of age to take up the heritage of our fathers. The Common Law, here and in England and round the world, looks to your youth and strength to improve it as good husbandmen. Remember that you are servants of the commonwealth, and are devoted not to a trade but to a science. Remember that the law of which we are ministers is a law of the courts and of the people; remember that its vital competence to satisfy the needs of the modern state is fed from its ancient Germanic roots of publicity and independence. Remember that if writs run in the name of King Edward VII. from the North Sea to the Pacific, it is largely because King Edward I. was a faithful servant of his people and of the law. Remember that it is your office as lawyers to give authentic form to the highest public morality of which you are capable as citizens, and that this office belongs of right no less to the bar than to the bench. Remember that our spiritual fellowship transcends political boundaries, and is as world-wide as our profession is honourable and its traditions venerable. Remember that our lady the Common Law is not a task-mistress but a bountiful sovereign whose service is freedom. The destinies of the English-speaking world are bound up with her fortune and her migrations, and its conquests are justified by her works. My words are over, and for any life to come they must look to your deeds. The empire of the Common Law is in your hands.

APPENDIX.

ENGLISH LAW BEFORE THE NORMAN CONQUEST.

[*First published in the "Law Quarterly Review,"* xiv. 291.]

ANGLO-SAXON life was rough and crude as compared not only with any modern standard but with the amount of civilization which survived, or had been recovered, on the Continent. There was very little foreign trade, not much internal traffic, nothing like industrial business of any kind on a large scale, and (it need hardly be said) no system of credit. Such conditions gave no room for refined legal science applied by elaborate legal machinery, such as those of the Roman Empire had been and those of modern England and the commonwealths that have sprung from her were to be. Such as the men were, such had to be the rules and methods whereby some kind of order was kept among them. Our ancestors before the Norman Conquest lived under a judicial system, if system it can be called, as rudimentary in substance as it was cumbrous in form. They sought justice, as a rule, at their primary local court, the court of the hundred, which met once a month, and for greater matters at a higher and more general court, the county court, which met only twice a year (*a*).

(*a*) There were probably intermediate meetings for merely formal business, which only a small number of the suitors attended: see P. & M. Hist. Eng. L. i. 526.

We say purposely met rather than sat. The courts were open-air meetings of the freemen who were bound to attend them, the *suitors* as they are called in the terms of Anglo-Norman and later medieval law; there was no class of professional lawyers; there were no judges in our sense of learned persons specially appointed to preside, expound the law, and cause justice to be done; the only learning available was that of the bishops, abbots, and other great ecclesiastics. This learning, indeed, was all the more available and influential because, before the Norman Conquest, there were no separate ecclesiastical courts in England. There were no clerks nor, apparently, any permanent officials of the popular courts; their judgments proceeded from the meeting itself, not from its presiding officer, and were regularly preserved only in the memory of the suitors. A modern student or man of business will at first sight wonder how this rude and scanty provision for judicial affairs can have sufficed even in the Dark Ages. But when we have reflected on the actual state of Anglo-Saxon society, we may be apt to think that at times the hundred and the county court found too little to do rather than too much. The materials for what we now call civil business practically did not exist.

There is now no doubt among scholars that the primary court was the hundred court. If the township had any regular meeting (which is quite uncertain), that meeting was not a judicial body. The king, on the other hand, assisted by his council of wise men, the Witan (*b*), had a superior authority in reserve. It was allowable to seek justice at the king's hands if one had failed, after due diligence, to obtain it in the hundred or the county court. Moreover, the Witan assumed jurisdiction in the first instance where land granted by the king was in question, and perhaps in other cases where religious foundations or the king's great men were concerned. Several examples of such proceedings are recorded, recited as

(*b*) There is more authority for this short form than for the fuller Witena-Gemót (not witenágemot as sometimes mispronounced by persons ignorant of old-English inflexions).

we should say in modern technical speech, in extant land-charters which declare and confirm the result of disputes, and therefore we know more of them than we do of the ordinary proceedings in the county and hundred courts, of which no written record was kept. But they can have had very little bearing, if any, on the daily lives of the smaller folk. In important cases the county court might be strengthened by adding the chief men of other counties; and, when thus reinforced, there is hardly anything to distinguish it from the Witan save that the king is not there in person (*c*).

Some considerable time before the Norman Conquest, but how long is not known, bishops and other great men had acquired the right of holding courts of their own and taking the profits in the shape of fines and fees, or what would have been the king's share of the profits. My own belief is that this began very early, but there is no actual proof of it. Twenty years after the Conquest, at any rate, we find private jurisdiction constantly mentioned in the Domesday Survey, and common in every part of England: about the same time, or very shortly afterwards, it was recognized as a main ingredient in the complex and artificial system of feudalism. After having grown in England, as elsewhere, to the point of threatening the king's supremacy, but having happily found in Edward I. a master such as it did not find elsewhere before the time of Richelieu, the manorial court is still with us in a form attenuated almost to the point of extinction. It is not material for the later history of English law to settle exactly how far the process of concession or encroachment had gone in the time of Edward the Confessor, or how fast its rate was increasing at the date of the Conquest. There can be no doubt that on the one hand it had gained and was gaining speed before "the day when King Edward was alive and dead" (*d*), or on the other hand that it was further accelerated

(*c*) Such a court, after the Conquest, was that which restored and confirmed the rights of the see of Canterbury on Penenden Heath; but it was held under a very special writ from the King.

(*d*) The common form of reference in Domesday Book.

and emphasized under rulers who were familiar with a more advanced stage of feudalism on the Continent. But this very familiarity helped to make them wise in time; and there was at least some foreshadowing of royal supremacy in existing English institutions. Although the courts of the hundred and the county were not the king's courts, the king was bound by his office to exercise some general supervision over their working. He was represented in the county court by the sheriff; he might send out commissioners to inquire and report how justice was done, though he could not interfere with the actual decisions. The efficiency of these powers varied in fact according to the king's means and capacity for exercising them. Under a wise and strong ruler like Alfred or Æthelstan they might count for much; under a feeble one like Æthelred they could count for very little.

A modern reader fresh to the subject might perhaps expect to find that the procedure of the old popular courts was loose and informal. In fact it was governed by traditional rules of the most formal and unbending kind (*e*). Little as we know of the details, we know enough to be sure of this; and it agrees with all the evidences we have of the early history of legal proceedings elsewhere. The forms become not less but more stringent as we pursue them to a higher antiquity; they seem to have not more but less appreciable relation to any rational attempt to ascertain the truth in disputed matters of fact. That task, indeed, appears to have been regarded as too hard or too dangerous to be attempted by unassisted human faculties. All the accustomed modes of proof involved some kind of appeal to supernatural sanctions. The simplest was the oath of one of the parties, not by way of testimony to particular facts, but by way of assertion of his whole claim or defence; and this was fortified by the oaths of a greater or less number of helpers, according to the nature of the case

(*e*) There were variations in the practice of different counties after the Conquest (Glanv. xii. 23), and therefore, almost certainly, before. We know nothing of their character or importance, but I should conjecture that they were chiefly in verbal formulas.

and the importance of the persons concerned, who swore with him that his oath was true (*f*). He lost his cause without a chance of recovery if any slip was made in pronouncing the proper forms, or if a sufficient number of helpers were not present and ready to make the oath. On the other hand the oath, like all archaic forms of proof, was conclusive when once duly carried through. Hence it was almost always an advantage to be called upon to make the oath of proof, and this usually belonged to the defendant. "Gainsaying is ever stronger than affirming . . . . . Owning is nearer to him who has the thing than to him who claims" (*g*). Our modern phrase "burden of proof" is quite inapplicable to the course of justice in Anglo-Saxon courts: the benefit or "prerogative" of proof, as it is called even in modern Scottish books, was eagerly contended for. The swearer and his oath-helpers might perjure themselves, but if they did there was no remedy for the loser in this world, unless he was prepared to charge the court itself with giving false judgment. Obviously there was no room in such a scheme for what we now call rules of evidence. Rules there were, but they declared what number of oath-helpers was required, or how many common men's oaths would balance a thegn's. In the absence of manifest facts, such as a fresh wound, which could be shown to the court, an oath called the "fore-oath" was required of the complainant in the first instance as a security against frivolous suits. This was quite different from the final oath of proof.

Oath being the normal mode of proof in disputes about property, we find it supplemented by ordeal in criminal accusations. A man of good repute could usually clear himself by oath; but circumstances of grave suspicion in the particular case, or previous bad character, would drive the defendant to stand his trial by ordeal. In the usual forms of which we read

(*f*) Advanced students will observe that this is wholly different from the decisory oath of Roman and modern Romanized procedure, where one party has the option of tendering the oath to the other alone, and is bound by the result.

(*g*) Æthelr. ii. 9.

in England the tests were sinking or floating in cold water (*h*), and recovery within a limited time, or rather healthy progress in recovery, from the effects of plunging the arm into boiling water or handling red-hot iron. The hot-water ordeal at any rate was in use from an early time, though the extant forms of ritual, after the Church had assumed the direction of the proceedings, are comparatively late. Originally, no doubt, the appeal was to the god of water or fire, as the case might be. The Church objected, temporized, hallowed the obstinate heathen customs by the addition of Christian ceremonies, and finally, but not until the thirteenth century, was strong enough to banish them. As a man was not put to the ordeal unless he was disqualified from clearing himself by oath for one of the reasons above mentioned, the results were probably less remote from rough justice than we should expect, and it seems that the proportion of acquittals was also larger. Certainly people generally believed to be guilty did often escape, how far accidentally or otherwise we can only conjecture (*i*). Another form of ordeal favoured in many Germanic tribes from early times, notwithstanding protest from the Church, and in use for deciding every kind of dispute, was trial by battle: but this makes its first appearance in England and Scotland not as a Saxon but as a distinctly Norman institution (*k*). It is hard to say why, but the fact is so. It seems from Anglo-Norman evidence that a party to a dispute which we should now call purely civil sometimes offered to prove his case not only by oath or combat, but by ordeal, as the court might award. This again suggests various explanations of which none is certain (*l*).

(*h*) There is a curious French variant of the cold-water ordeal in which not the accused person, but some bystander taken at random, is immersed: I do not know of any English example.

(*i*) The cold-water ordeal was apparently most feared; see the case of Ailward, Materials for Hist. St. Thomas, i. 156, ii. 172; Bigelow, Plac. A.-N. 260. For a full account, see Lea, Superstition and Force.

(*k*) See more in Neilson, Trial by Combat.

(*l*) Cases from D. B. collected in Bigelow, Plac. A.-N., 40—44, 61.

Inasmuch as all the early modes of proof involved large elements of unknown risk, it was rather common for the parties to compromise at the last moment. Also, since there were no ready means of enforcing the performance of a judgment on unwilling parties, great men supported by numerous followers could often defy the court, and this naturally made it undesirable to carry matters to extremity which, if both parties were strong, might mean private war. Most early forms of jurisdiction, indeed, of which we have any knowledge, seem better fitted to put pressure on the litigants to agree than to produce an effective judgment of compulsory force. Assuredly this was the case with those which we find in England even after the consolidation of the kingdom under the Danish dynasty.

Rigid and cumbrous as Anglo-Saxon justice was in the things it did provide for, it was, to modern eyes, strangely defective in its lack of executive power. Among the most important functions of courts as we know them is compelling the attendance of parties and enforcing the fulfilment both of final judgments and of interlocutory orders dealing with the conduct of proceedings and the like. Such things are done as of course under the ordinary authority of the court, and with means constantly at its disposal; open resistance to judicial orders is so plainly useless that it is seldom attempted, and obstinate preference of penalties to submission, a thing which now and then happens, is counted a mark of eccentricity bordering on unsoundness of mind. Exceptional difficulties, when they occur, indicate an abnormal state of the commonwealth or some of its members. But this reign of law did not come by nature; it has been slowly and laboriously won. Jurisdiction began, it seems, with being merely voluntary, derived not from the authority of the State but from the consent of the parties. People might come to the court for a

Even under Henry II. we find, in terms, such an offer, but it looks, in the light of the context, more like a rhetorical asseveration—in fact the modern "j'en mettrais ma main au feu"—than anything else: *op. cit.* 196.

decision if they agreed to do so. They were bound in honour to accept the result; they might forfeit pledges deposited with the court; but the court could not compel their obedience any more than a tribunal of arbitration appointed at this day under a treaty between sovereign States can compel the rulers of those States to fulfil its award. Anglo-Saxon courts had got beyond this most early stage, but not very far beyond it.

The only way to bring an unwilling adversary before the court was to take something of his as security till he would attend to the demand; and practically the only things that could be taken without personal violence were cattle. Distress in this form was practised and also regulated from a very early time. It was forbidden to distrain until right had been formally demanded—in Cnut's time to the extent of three summonings—and refused. Thus leave of the court was required, but the party had to act for himself as best he could. If distress failed to make the defendant appear, the only resource left was to deny the law's protection to the stiff-necked man who would not come to be judged by law. He might be outlawed, and this must have been enough to coerce most men who had anything to lose and were not strong enough to live in rebellion; but still no right could be done to the complainant without his submission. The device of a judgment by default, which is familiar enough to us, was unknown, and probably would not have been understood.

Final judgment, when obtained, could in like manner not be directly enforced. The successful party had to see to gathering the "fruits of judgment," as we say, for himself. In case of continued refusal to do right according to the sentence of the court, he might take the law into his own hands, in fact wage war on his obstinate opponent. The ealdorman's aid, and ultimately the king's, could be invoked in such extreme cases as that of a wealthy man, or one backed by a powerful family, setting the law at open defiance. But this was an extraordinary measure, analogous to nothing in the regular modern process of law.

The details of Anglo-Saxon procedure and judicial usage

had become or were fast becoming obsolete in the thirteenth century, which is as much as to say that they were already outworn when the definite growth of the Common Law began. But the general features of the earlier practice, and still more the ideas that underlay them, have to be borne in mind. They left their stamp on the course of our legal history in manifold ways; many things in the medieval law cannot be understood without reference to them; and even in modern law their traces are often to be found.

While the customary forms of judgment and justice were such as we have said, there was a comparatively large amount of legislation or at least express declaration of law; and, what is even more remarkable, it was delivered in the mother tongue of the people from the first. Æthelberht, the converted king of Kent, was anxious to emulate the civilization of Rome in secular things also, and reduced the customs of his kingdom, so far as might be, to writing; but they were called *dooms*, not *leges*; they were issued in English, and were translated into Latin only after the lapse of some centuries. Other Kentish princes, and afterwards Ine of Wessex, followed the example; but the regular series of Anglo-Saxon laws begins towards the end of the ninth century with Alfred's publication of his own dooms, and (it seems) an amended version of Ine's, in which these are now preserved. Through the century and a half between Alfred's time and Cnut's (*m*) legislation was pretty continuous, and it was always in English. The later restoration of English to the statute roll after the medieval reign of Latin and French was not the new thing it seemed. It may be that the activity of the Wessex princes in legislation was connected with the conquest of the Western parts of England, and the need of having fixed rules for the conduct of affairs in the newly settled districts. No one doubts that a considerable West-Welsh population remained in this

(*m*) The so-called laws of Edward the Confessor, an antiquarian compilation of the twelfth century largely mixed with invention, do not even profess to be actual dooms of the Confessor, but the customs of his time collected by order of William the Conqueror.

region, and it would have been difficult to apply any local West-Saxon custom to them.

Like all written laws, the Anglo-Saxon dooms have to be interpreted in the light of their circumstances. Unluckily for modern students, the matters of habit and custom which they naturally take for granted are those of which we now have least direct evidence. A large part of them is filled by minute catalogues of the fines and compositions payable for manslaughter, wounding, and other acts of violence. We may well suppose that in matters of sums and number such provisions often express an authoritative compromise between the varying though not widely dissimilar usages of local courts; at all events we have an undoubted example of a like process in the fixing of standard measures after the Conquest; and in some of the later Anglo-Saxon laws we get a comparative standard of Danish and English reckoning. Otherwise we cannot certainly tell how much is declaration of existing custom, or what we should now call consolidation, and how much was new. We know from Alfred's preamble to his laws, evidently framed with special care, that he did innovate to some extent, but, like a true father of English statesmen, was anxious to innovate cautiously. On the whole the Anglo-Saxon written laws, though of priceless use to students of the times, need a good deal of circumspection and careful comparison of other authorities for using them aright. It is altogether misleading to speak of them as codes, or as if they were intended to be a complete exposition of the customary law.

We pass on to the substance of Anglo-Saxon law, so far as capable of being dealt with in a summary view. There were sharp distinctions between different conditions of persons, noble, free, and slave. We may talk of "serfs" if we like, but the Anglo-Saxon "theow" was much more like a Roman slave than a medieval villein. Not only slaves could be bought and sold, but there was so much regular slave-trading that selling men beyond seas had to be specially forbidden. Slaves were more harshly punished than free men, and must have been largely at their owner's mercy, though there is reason to think that usage had a more advanced standard of humanity than was afforded by any positive rules. Manumission was not uncommon, and was specially favoured by the Church. The slave had opportunities (perhaps first secured under Alfred) for acquiring means of his own, and sometimes bought his freedom.

Among free men there were two kinds of difference. A man might be a lord having dependents, protecting them and in turn supported by them, and answerable in some measure for their conduct; or he might be a free man of small estate dependent on a lord. In the tenth century, if not before, every man who was not a lord himself was bound to have a lord on pain of being treated as unworthy of a free man's rights; "lordless man" was to Anglo-Saxon ears much the same as "rogue and vagabond" to ours. This wide-spread relation of lord and man was one of the elements that in due time went to make up feudalism. It was not necessarily associated with any holding of land by the man from the lord, but the association was doubtless already common a long time before the Conquest, and there is every reason to think that the legally uniform class of dependent free men included many varieties of wealth and prosperity. Many were probably no worse off than substantial farmers, and many not much better than slaves.

The other legal difference between free men was their estimation for *wergild*, the "man's price" which a man's kinsfolk were entitled to demand from his slayer, and which sometimes he might have to pay for his own offences; and this was the more important because the weight of a man's oath also varied with it. A *thegn* (which would be more closely represented by "gentilhomme" than by "nobleman") had a wergild six times as great as a *ceorl's* (*n*) or common man's, and his oath counted for six common oaths before the

(*n*) The modern forms of these words, *thane* and *churl*, have passed through so much change of meaning and application that they cannot be safely used for historical purposes.

court (*o*). All free men, noble or simple, looked to their kindred as their natural helpers and avengers; and one chief office of early criminal law was to regulate the blood-feud until there was a power strong enough to supersede it.

We collect from the general tenor of the Anglo-Saxon laws that the evils most frequently calling for remedy were man-slaying, wounding, and cattle-stealing; it is obvious enough that the latter, when followed by pursuit in hot blood, was a natural and prolific source of the two former. The rules dealing with such wrongs or crimes (for archaic laws draw no firm line between public offence and private injury) present a strange contrast of crude ideas and minute specification, as it appears at first sight. Both are however really due to similar conditions. A society which is incapable of refined conceptions, but is advanced enough to require equal rules of some kind and to limit the ordinary power of its rulers, is likewise incapable of leaving any play for judicial discretion. Anglo-Saxon courts had not the means of apportioning punishment to guilt in the particular case, or assessing compensation according to the actual damage, any more than of deciding on the merits of conflicting claims according to the evidence. Thus the only way remaining open was to fix an equivalent in money or in kind for each particular injury: so much for life and so much for every limb and member of the human body. The same thing occurs with even greater profusion of detail in the other Germanic compilations of the Dark Ages. In the latter days of Anglo-Saxon monarchy treason was added to the rude catalogue of crimes, under continental influence ultimately derived from Roman law; but the sin of plotting against the sovereign was the more readily conceived as heinous above all others by reason of the ancient Germanic principle of faith between a lord and his men. This prominence of the personal relation explains why down

(*o*) There were minor distinctions between ranks of free men which are now obscure, and were probably no less obscure in the thirteenth century: they seem to have been disregarded very soon after the Conquest.

to quite modern times the murder of a husband by his wife, of a master by his servant, and of an ecclesiastical superior by a clerk, secular or regular, owing him obedience, were specially classed as "petit treason" and distinguished from murder in general (*p*).

Secret murder as opposed to open slaying was treated with special severity. This throws no light on our later criminal law; nor has it much to do with love of a fair fight, though this may have strengthened the feeling; rather it goes back to a time when witchcraft, and poisoning as presumably connected therewith, were believed to be unavoidable by ordinary caution, and regarded with a supernatural horror which is still easy to observe among barbarous people. With these exceptions, and a few later ones of offences reserved for the king's jurisdiction, crimes were not classified or distinguished in Anglo-Saxon custom save by the amount of public fine (*q*) and private composition required to redeem the wrong-doer's life in each case. Capital punishment and money payment, or rather liability to the blood-feud redeemable by money payment, and slavery for a thief who could not make the proper fine, were the only means of compulsion generally applicable, though false accusers and some other infamous persons were liable to corporal penalties. Imprisonment is not heard of as a substantive punishment; and it is needless to say that nothing like a system of penal discipline was known. We cannot doubt that a large number of offences, even notorious ones, went unpunished. The more skilled and subtle attacks on property, such as forgery and allied kinds of fraud, did not occur, not because men were more honest, but because fraudulent documents could not be invented or employed in a society which knew nothing of credit and did not use writing for any common business of life.

(*p*) Bl. Com. iv. 203.

(*q*) *Wite* was probably, in its origin, rather a fee to the court for arranging the composition than a punishment. But it is treated as penal from the earliest period of written laws. In the tenth century it could mean pain or torment; see C. D. 1222 *ad fin.*

Far more significant for the future development of English law are the beginnings of the King's Peace. In later times this became a synonym for public order maintained by the king's general authority; nowadays we do not easily conceive how the peace which lawful men ought to keep can be any other than the King's or the commonwealth's. But the king's justice, as we have seen, was at first not ordinary but exceptional, and his power was called to aid only when other means had failed. To be in the king's peace was to have a special protection, a local or personal privilege. Every free man was entitled to peace in his own house, the sanctity of the homestead being one of the most ancient and general principles of Teutonic law. The worth set on a man's peace, like that of his life, varied with his rank, and thus the king's peace was higher than any other man's. Fighting in the king's house was a capital offence from an early time. Gradually the privileges of the king's house were extended to the precincts of his court, to the army, to the regular meetings of the shire and hundred, and to the great roads. Also the king might grant special personal protection to his officers and followers; and these two kinds of privilege spread until they coalesced and covered the whole ground. The more serious public offences were appropriated to the king's jurisdiction; the king's peace was used as a special sanction for the settlement of blood-feuds, and was proclaimed on various solemn occasions; it seems to have been specially prominent—may we say as a "frontier regulation"?—where English conquest and settlement were recent (*r*). In the generation before the Conquest it was, to all appearance, extending fast. In this kind of development the first stage is a really exceptional right; the second is a right which has to be distinctly claimed, but is open to all who will claim it in the proper form; the third is the "common right" which the courts will take for granted. The Normans found the king's peace nearing, if not touching, the second stage.

(*r*) See the customs of Chester, D. B. i. 262 b, extracted in Stubbs, Sel. Ch.

Except for a few peculiar provisions, there is nothing in Anglo-Saxon customs resembling our modern distinctions between wilful, negligent, and purely accidental injuries. Private vengeance does not stop to discriminate in such matters, and customary law which started from making terms with the avenger could not afford to take a more judicial view. This old harshness of the Germanic rules has left its traces in the Common Law down to quite recent times. A special provision in Alfred's laws recommends a man carrying a spear on his shoulder to keep the point level with the butt; if another runs on the point so carried, only simple compensation at most (*s*) will be payable. If the point has been borne higher (so that it would naturally come in a man's face), this carelessness may put the party to his oath to avoid a fine. If a dog worried or killed any one, the owner was answerable in a scale of fines rising after the first offence (*t*); the indulgence of the modern law which requires knowledge of the dog's habits was unknown. But it may be doubted whether these rules applied to anything short of serious injury. Alfred's wise men show their practical sense by an explanatory caution which they add: the owner may not set up as an excuse that the dog forthwith ran away and was lost. This might otherwise have seemed an excellent defence according to the archaic notion that the animal or instrument which does damage carries the liability about with it, and the owner may free himself by abandoning it (*noxa caput sequitur*) (*u*).

We have spoken of money payments for convenience; but it does not seem likely that enough money was available, as a rule, to pay the more substantial wergilds and fines; and it must once have been the common practice for the pacified avenger to accept cattle, arms, or valuable ornaments, at a price agreed between the parties or settled by the court.

(*s*) Ælf. 36. The statement is rather obscure.

(*t*) Ælf. 23.

(*u*) See Holmes, The Common Law, 7—12.

The alternative of delivering cattle is expressly mentioned in some of the earlier laws.

As for the law of property, it was rudimentary, and inextricably mixed up with precautions against theft and charges of theft. A prudent buyer of cattle had to secure himself against the possible claim of some former owner who might allege that the beasts had been stolen. The only way to do this was to take every step in public and with good witness. If he set out on a journey to a fair, he would let his neighbours know it. When he did business either far or near, he would buy only in open market and before credible persons, and, if the sale were at any distance from home, still more if he had done some trade on the way without having set out for the purpose, he would call the good men of his own township to witness when he came back driving his newly-gotten oxen, and not till then would he turn them out on the common pasture. These observances, probably approved by long-standing custom, are prescribed in a whole series of ordinances on pain of stringent forfeitures (*x*). Even then a purchaser whose title was challenged had to produce his seller, or, if he could not do that, clear himself by oath. The seller might produce in turn the man from whom he had bought, and he again might do the like; but this process ("vouching to warranty" in the language of later medieval law) could not be carried more than three steps back, to the "fourth hand" including the buyer himself. All this has nothing to do with the proof of the contract in case of a dispute between the original parties to the sale; it is much more aimed at collusion between them, in fact at arrangements for the receipt and disposal of stolen goods. The witnesses to the sale are there not for the parties' sake, but as a check in the public interest. We are tempted at first sight to think of various modern enactments that require signature or other formalities as a condition of particular kinds of contracts being enforceable; but their provisions belong to a wholly different category.

(*x*) See especially Edg. iv. 6—11.

Another archaic source of anxiety is that borrowed arms may be used in a fatal fight and bring the lender into trouble. The early notion would be that a weapon used for manslaying should bring home the liability with it to the owner, quite regardless of any fault; which would afterwards become a more or less rational presumption that he lent it for no good purpose. Then the risk of such weapons being forfeited continued down to modern times. Hence the armourer who takes a sword or spear to be repaired, and even a smith who takes charge of tools, must warrant their return free from blood-guiltiness, unless it has been agreed to the contrary (*y*). We also find, with regard to the forfeiture of things which "move to death," that even in case of pure accident, such as a tree falling on a woodman, the kindred still have their rights. They may take away the tree if they will come for it within thirty days (*z*).

There was not any law of contract at all, as we now understand it. The two principal kinds of transaction requiring the exchange or acceptance of promises to be performed in the future were marriage and the payment of wergild. Apart from the general sanctions of the Church, and the king's special authority where his peace had been declared, the only ways of adding any definite security to a promise were oath and giving of pledges. One or both of these were doubtless regularly used on solemn occasions like the settlement of a blood-feud; and we may guess that the oath, which at all events carried a spiritual sanction, was freely resorted to for various purposes. But business had hardly got beyond delivery against ready money between parties both present, and there was not much room for such confidence as that on which, for example, the existence of modern banking rests. How far the popular law took any notice of petty trading disputes, such as there were, we are not informed; it seems likely that for the most part they were left to be settled by special customs of traders, and possibly by special local

(*y*) Ælf. 19. (*z*) Ælf. 13.

tribunals in towns and markets. Merchants trafficking beyond seas, in any case, must have relied on the customs of their trade and order rather than the cumbrous formal justice of the time.

Anglo-Saxon landholding has been much discussed, but is still imperfectly understood, and our knowledge of it, so far from throwing any light on the later law, depends largely on what can be inferred from Anglo-Norman sources. It is certain that there were a considerable number of independent free men holding land of various amounts down to the time of the Conquest. In the eastern counties some such holdings, undoubtedly free, were very small indeed (*a*). But many of the lesser free men were in practical subjection to a lord who was entitled to receive dues and services from them; he got a share of their labour in tilling his land, rents in money and kind, and so forth. In short they were already in much the same position as those who were called villeins in the twelfth and thirteenth centuries. Also some poor free men seem to have hired themselves out to work for others from an early time (*b*). We know next to nothing of the rules under which free men, whether of greater or lesser substance, held "folk-land," that is, estates governed by the old customary law. Probably there was not much buying and selling of such land. There is no reason to suppose that alienation was easier than in other archaic societies, and some local customs found surviving long after the Conquest point to the conclusion that often the consent of the village as well as of the family was a necessary condition of a sale. Indeed it is not certain that folk-land, generally speaking, could be sold at all. There is equally no reason to think that ordinary free landholders could dispose of their land by will, or were in the habit of making wills for any purpose. Anglo-Saxon wills (or rather documents more like a modern will than a modern deed) exist, but they are the wills of great folk, such as were accustomed to witness the king's charters, had their

(*a*) Maitland, Domesday Book and Beyond, 106. (*b*) Ælf. 43.

own wills witnessed or confirmed by bishops and kings, and held charters of their own; and it is by no means clear that the lands dealt with in these wills were held as ordinary folk-land. In some cases it looks as if a special licence or consent had been required; we also hear of persistent attempts by the heirs to dispute even gifts to great churches (*c*).

Soon after the conversion of the south of England to Christianity, English kings began to grant the lordship and revenues of lands, often of extensive districts, to the Church, or more accurately speaking to churches, by written charters framed in imitation of continental models. Land held under these grants by charter or "book," which in course of time acquired set forms and characters peculiar to England, was called *bookland*, and the king's bounty in this kind was in course of time extended to his lay magnates. The same extraordinary power of the king, exercised with the witness and advice (*d*) of his witan, which could confer a title to princely revenues, could also confer large disposing capacities unknown to the customary law; thus the fortunate holder of bookland might be and often was entitled not only to make a grant in his lifetime or to let it on such terms as he chose, but also to leave it by will. My own belief is that the land given by the Anglo-Saxon wills which are preserved was almost always bookland even when it is not so described. Indeed these wills are rather in the nature of postponed grants, as in Scotland a "trust disposition" had to be till quite lately, than of a true last will and testament as we now understand it. They certainly had nothing to do with the Roman testament (*e*).

Long before the Conquest it had become the ambition of every man of substance to hold bookland, and we may well think that this was on the way to become the normal form of

(*c*) See C. D. 226 compared with 256.

(*d*) A strictly accurate statement in few words is hardly possible. See the section "Book-land and Folk-land" in Maitland, Domesday Book and Beyond, p. 244 *sqq.*

(*e*) See P. & M., Hist. Eng. L., bk. II. c. vi. § 3.

land-ownership. But this process, whatever its results might have been, was broken off by the advent of Norman lords and Norman clerks with their own different set of ideas and forms.

The various customs of inheritance that are to be found even to this day in English copyholds, and to a limited extent in freehold land, and which are certainly of great antiquity, bear sufficient witness that at least as much variety was to be found before the Conquest. Probably the least usual of the typical customs was primogeniture; preference of the youngest son, ultimogeniture or junior-right as recent authors have called it, the "borough-English" of our post-Norman books, was common in some parts; preference of the youngest daughter, in default of sons, or even of the youngest among collateral heirs, was not unknown. But the prevailing type was equal division among sons, not among children including daughters on an equal footing as modern systems have it. Here again the effect of the Norman Conquest was to arrest or divert the native lines of growth. In England we now live under laws of succession derived in part from the military needs of Western Europe in the early Middle Ages, and in part from the cosmopolitan legislation of Justinian, the line between the application of the two systems being drawn in a manner which is accounted for by the peculiar history of our institutions and the relations between different jurisdictions, but cannot be explained on any rational principle. But the unlimited freedom of disposal by will which we enjoy under our modern law has reduced the anomalies of our intestate succession to a matter of only occasional inconvenience.

Small indeed, it is easy to perceive, is the portion of Anglo-Saxon customs which can be said to have survived in a recognizable form. This fact nevertheless remains compatible with a perfectly real and living continuity of spirit in our legal institutions.

INDEX.

PRINTED BY C. F. ROWORTH, GREAT NEW STREET, FETTER LANE, E.C.